USBORNE BOOK OF
WINDSURFING

Janet Cook and Penny Way

Consultant: Tim Wills (RYA windsurfing

Designed by Nerissa Davies

Additional design by Christopher Gillingwate

Illustrated by John Beswick, Kuo Kang Chen
and Susan Alcantarilla

Cover illustration by Mick Posen and Chris Lyon

Photographers: Bob Martin (All-Sport UK) and Rob Jewell

Editorial assistance from Felicity Everett
and Constance Novis

**Photographs taken on location in
Ithaca and Barbados with the help of the
Greek Island Sailing Club and the Barbados Tourist Board**

Contents

First published in 1988 by Usborne Publishing Ltd, Usborne House, 83-85 Saffron Hill, London EC1N 8RT, England.

Using this book

The techniques explained in this book are illustrated step-by-step with photographs. Each photograph has a small arrow printed on it, to indicate where the wind is coming from. When learning a new manoeuvre, try to memorize the whole sequence before going out on the water to try it out for yourself.

Don't worry if you keep falling into the water: everyone does at first. If you have difficulties, refer to the problem boxes. These cover the most common mistakes made by beginners, and suggest key points to remember when you try again.

Many newcomers to the sport are totally confused by the theory. For example, why should the board turn into the wind when you lean the rig towards the back of the board? And why do experts change the position of the daggerboard and mast foot to suit different courses and wind conditions? This book provides clear answers to such questions as they

Freestyling

Wave jumping

Racing

arise. By understanding the theory, you will find it easier to master the technique on the water.

Once you have the basic skills, you may wish to try your hand at one of the three advanced windsurfing specialities shown on the left. These include freestyling (for those who are agile on their boards, but don't necessarily enjoy sailing in very strong winds), racing (for those with a competitive streak), or waveriding and jumping (for the really adventurous). The book gives you a taste of each of these, and suggests good books to read if you wish to develop your skills further.

Most people either borrow or hire equipment for their first attempts at windsurfing. For this reason, the book starts by explaining technique, rather than giving advice on buying and looking after windsurfing equipment at the start. For this information, you should refer to pages 46-57.

About Penny Way

Penny Way started windsurfing in 1980 and was competing within five weeks of first standing on the board. She won her first national championship in 1981 and has held at least one national title every year since then. Other trophies include:

1983 Holder of the British speed record.
1984 Winner of the Mistral European Championships and holder of the British speed record.
1985 Member of the winning team at the National Team Racing Championships, and holder of the British speed record.
1986 Member of the winning team at the National Team Racing Championships and winner of the Women's World Championships.

Besides competing, she helped to set up a windsurfing shop in Australia and ran a windsurfing school in New Zealand. She qualified as a Royal Yachting Association instructor in 1986 and runs improver courses in a number of countries. Her involvement in the windsurfing industry includes designing and promoting wetsuits and leisurewear for Javlin.

A look at the windsurfer

One of the great advantages that windsurfers have over other sailing craft is their simplicity. You can transport them on the roof of a car (see pages 56-57), and rig up in less than 20 minutes (see pages 54-55).

Today's windsurfer is very different from those of the 1960s. New materials and design ideas are enabling manufacturers to produce more efficient and long-lasting boards and sails every year. You can find out more about the most up-to-date board and sail designs on pages 46-49.

Naming the parts

The picture on the right shows all the parts of the windsurfer, giving their names and explaining their functions. You will probably find it a very useful source of reference when you are first learning the sport.

The sail, mast and boom are collectively known as the rig.

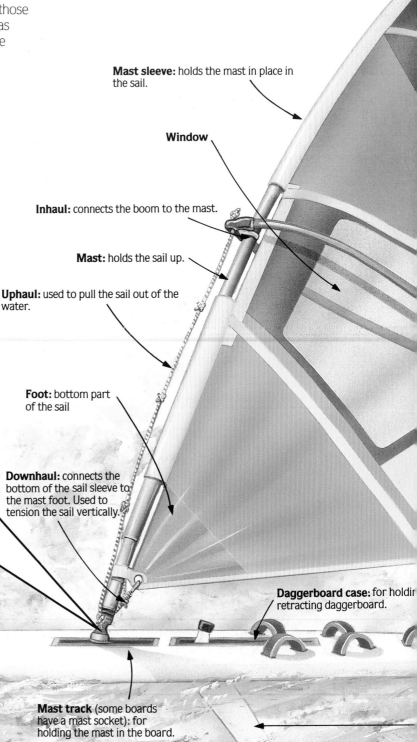

Mast sleeve: holds the mast in place in the sail.

Window

Inhaul: connects the boom to the mast.

Mast: holds the sail up.

Uphaul: used to pull the sail out of the water.

Mast foot: connects the mast to the mast track or socket. Includes a flexible joint (the universal joint) which allows you to tilt the mast at any angle.

Universal joint

Foot: bottom part of the sail

Downhaul: connects the bottom of the sail sleeve to the mast foot. Used to tension the sail vertically.

Towing eye: to hold a towing rope, if necessary.

Daggerboard case: for holdi retracting daggerboard.

Nose of the board

Rails: edges of the board.

Mast track (some boards have a mast socket): for holding the mast in the board.

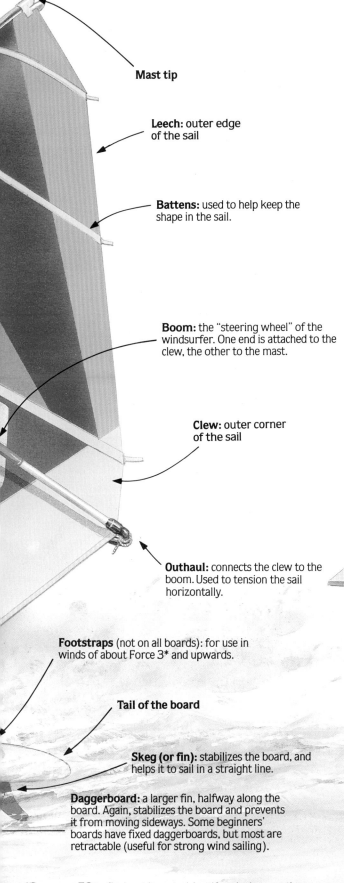

Mast tip

Leech: outer edge of the sail

Battens: used to help keep the shape in the sail.

Boom: the "steering wheel" of the windsurfer. One end is attached to the clew, the other to the mast.

Clew: outer corner of the sail

Outhaul: connects the clew to the boom. Used to tension the sail horizontally.

Footstraps (not on all boards): for use in winds of about Force 3* and upwards.

Tail of the board

Skeg (or fin): stabilizes the board, and helps it to sail in a straight line.

Daggerboard: a larger fin, halfway along the board. Again, stabilizes the board and prevents it from moving sideways. Some beginners' boards have fixed daggerboards, but most are retractable (useful for strong wind sailing).

The birth of the windsurfer

There have been many arguments, both in and out of court, about who 'invented' the windsurfer. The major feature that sets it apart from other sailing craft is that it is steered by means of its sail.

Probably the first people to design a sailing craft which could be steered without a rudder were the Indians. They manoeuvred their rafts up and down the Amazon by changing the position of the mast. The mast could be moved into any one of a number of different holes, embedded in the base of the raft (see right).

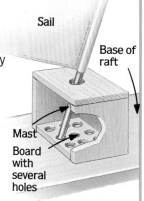

Sail

Base of raft

Mast

Board with several holes

In 1964, Mr Newman Darby developed a primitive form of windsurfer. It consisted of a rig similar in structure and shape to a kite. The mast could move backwards and forwards along the board, but apart from this, was fixed.

In 1965, an American magazine published an article on this new 'sailboard', announcing "A Sport So New That Fewer Than 10 People Have Mastered It".

Sail fixed to a cross-shaped frame.

Fixed mast

Fixed daggerboard

Although a few enthusiasts attempted to improve this design, it was not until 1968 that two Californians, Jim Drake and Hoyle Schweitzer, patented the prototype for today's windsurfer. It consisted of an ordinary surfboard (made of plastic foam covered with fibreglass) and a triangular sail. Its major breakthrough was the universal joint attached to the foot of the mast which enabled the rig to be moved in any direction.

Boom shaped like a wishbone.

Triangular sail

Flexible mast

Fixed daggerboard

Fin

Before you start

Before braving the water, it is well worth taking the time to ensure that you are properly prepared. Do you have the necessary clothing, and a board and rig suitable for a beginner? Will you be able to cope with the wind? Have you chosen a safe venue? Do you know what to do if you get into difficulties? Good preparation gives you confidence and enables you to learn quickly and safely.

Kitting yourself out

Below there are some tips on the basic clothing and equipment that you may need. You will find more detailed advice on how to choose between the wide range of items available on pages 46-51.

Wetsuit or drysuit

Unless you are windsurfing in very warm conditions, it is vital to wear a wetsuit or drysuit to protect yourself against the chilling effect of wind on your wet body. When you get cold, your body attempts to maintain its core temperature of 37°C through muscular spasms (shivering). When the heat produced by shivering fails to maintain the core temperature, the body's vital organs begin to fail. This is known as hypothermia.

Gloves and hats

Gloves and hats are essential in cold weather. 20% of body heat is lost through the head. Some people always wear gloves to prevent getting blisters.

Footwear

Plastic or rubber-soled shoes protect your feet and provide grip on the board. For cold weather, you need wetsuit boots or dip-coated socks (see page 51).

Buoyancy aid or life-jacket

Even if you are a strong swimmer, a rapid change in weather conditions could be fatal. Wearing a buoyancy aid or life-jacket will improve your chances of survival.* A buoyancy aid is less bulky than a life-jacket, and suitable for most conditions. However, if you are knocked unconscious, a life-jacket will keep your head above water. A buoyancy aid will not.

All-round board

Boom

Mast

Sail

Rig

The boom, sail and mast should be light, so that it is easy to pull them out of the water. The lighter the wind and the heavier you are, the larger the sail you need.

Board

The easiest board to learn on has a wide tail and is 360-380cm long. This gives maximum stability. However, as you progress, a beginner's board will seem sluggish and you will need a shorter, more advanced board. Alternatively, you could learn on an all-round board which is not so stable, but which you will not outgrow so quickly. Look for one which has footstraps (you can take them off until you are more advanced), an adjustable mast track (this can be locked in mid-position until you are ready to use it) and a fully retractable daggerboard (necessary for more advanced strong wind sailing).

*Some people use harnesses as buoyancy aids instead (see pages 24-25).

Choosing a place to sail

For your first attempts afloat, choose a small lake or reservoir. Make sure there are rescue facilities available and tell the rescue team that you are a beginner so that they know to keep an eye on you.

Once you feel more confident, you may wish to try sailing on the open sea. This is fun, but potentially dangerous unless you are aware of the hazards, such as strong tides (see page 59).

Self-rescue

Should your equipment break, or the conditions change, you may be unable to sail back to shore. Below are some other methods of returning to land: the one you use will depend on the

Safety tips

★ Always assess the strength and direction of the wind before sailing (see pages 58-59). Beginners should not sail in wind above Force 3. Never sail when it is directly offshore (blowing away from the shore) or onshore (blowing on to the shore).
★ Make sure there are others sailing near you.
★ Before you go out, choose a landmark on the shore as your base. Keep checking where it is in comparison to you – it is easy to lose your bearings.
★ Tell someone you are going out, and when you expect to return. Then tell them when you have returned.
★ Check your equipment is well rigged and in good condition (see page 55).
★ Make sure that you can cope in the conditions. Never sail in the dark or in foggy weather.
★ Always carry a safety pack (see page 50).
★ Familiarize yourself with the right of way rules outlined on page 59.
★ Don't become exhausted through sailing for too long.

strength and direction of the wind. As a last resort, signal for help by slowly waving your arms up and down by your sides. This is the International Distress Signal. Also, if you have a whistle, day-glo flag, or flare in your safety pack, use them. Whatever happens, stay with your board: it will keep you afloat, and make you more visible to rescuers.

Any wind

Sitting, unfasten the rig safety leash and remove the mast foot. Take out the battens, and slip them down your wetsuit.

Release the outhaul and push the end of the boom up to the top of the sail. Now tightly roll up the sail around the mast.

Tie the top half of the mast and sail together with the outhaul, and the bottom half with the uphaul. Lay the rig across the board.

Rotate the rig through 90°. If you have a loop attached to the towing eye of the board*, slip the mast foot through it.

Lie on the board and paddle to the nearest land. If the battens feel uncomfortable, push them between the uphaul and rig.

Light or no wind

Pull the rig over the back of the board. Lie on the board, holding the rig in place with your feet, and paddle for shore.

Medium or strong wind

To travel across the wind, stand with your back to the wind and pull the rig until it is partially clear of the water.

To travel with the wind (go downwind), pull the rig completely clear. Now turn to face the front of the board.

Getting started

One of the most important aspects of good windsurfing is the ability to balance well on the board and feel confident when moving around on it. Below are some exercises to do using just your board, without the rig. Once you have mastered these, you will find it easier to learn basic manoeuvres which involve both the board and the rig.*

On the next page you can find out how to pull the sail out of the water and position it in such a way that the board will not move.

Climbing on to the board

Put the board into thigh-deep water. Push the daggerboard fully down so that the knob is as far back as it will go.

Place your hands on the centreline of the board either side of the mast socket, approximately shoulder-width apart.

Push down on your hands and gently pull your body on to the board so that you are kneeling on the centreline just inside your hands.

Getting your balance

Now try the following exercises. You will probably fall off a lot at first but gradually you will become more stable.

1. Sitting, tip the board each way to see how it reacts to your body weight.

2. Pull yourself to your feet and stand up. Shuffle your feet sideways to the left, then to the right.

3. Face the front of the board and walk to the end. Turn around and walk to the other end, then back again.

4. Walk around the centre of the board in a complete circle.

5. Stand on one leg for 20 seconds, then on the other.

6. Now do some jumps – starting with a quarter jump (90°) then a half jump (180°) and finishing with a whole jump (360°).

Problem box

Problem You cannot keep your balance on the board and keep falling off, into the water.

Solution It is essential that your body-weight is over the centreline of the board. If your feet are to one side of the centreline, lean the rest of your body towards the centre of the board to compensate for them.

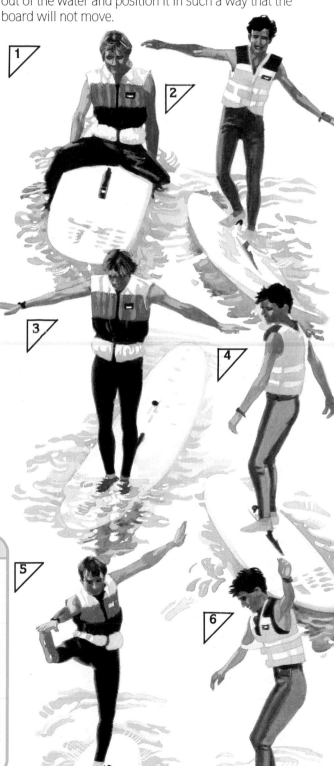

*See pages 56-57 for advice on launching your board and rig.

Lifting the sail up

Firstly, connect the rig to the board by placing the mast foot firmly in its slot and attaching the safety leash to the board. Position the board so that it is lying at right angles to the wind, with the rig facing away from the wind.

It is possible to injure your back by lifting the sail wrongly. The following technique will make your thighs take most of the strain. If you still feel a strain on your back, try to concentrate on keeping your bottom tucked in and your back as straight as possible.

Haul yourself into a kneeling position (see opposite). Take hold of the uphaul with one hand and leave the other hand free to help you balance.

Check the direction of the wind. If the board has moved from its 90° angle to the wind, climb off and start again. Now crouch on the board.

Still holding the uphaul, stand up. The rig should stay in the water. Keeping your back straight, bend your knees, then straighten them as you pull the uphaul taut.

Bend then extend your legs again, and pull the rig partially clear of the water. Let the water fall out of the sail and mast tube (this is the drain position).

Now bend your knees again and work hand over hand until the boom is clear of the water. Move your hands from the uphaul to the mast which is more stable.

Relax in this position, keeping your arms and legs slightly bent. The rig and your body should form a 'V' shape. Try to get used to the weight of the rig.

Now see how the board reacts to the movements of the rig. Lean the mast towards the back of the board, and feel the board's nose turn towards the wind.

To turn the nose away from the wind, lean the rig towards the front of the board. Finally, manoeuvre the board so that it is at right angles to the wind.

The secure position

The position you reached at the end of the sequence is the secure position; the wind travels either side of the sail, and the board cannot move off. If you are moving, make these checks:
★ Is the board still at right angles to the wind?
★ Is the wind coming from directly behind you?
★ Is the sail flapping straight ahead of you?

Wind   Wind

Lifting the sail with the wind in front of you

When you are windsurfing, you may well fall off the board and find that the rig is on the same side of the board as the wind (this is called the windward side). In this case, you have to manoeuvre the rig to the other side of the board (the leeward side). The easiest way to do this is to make the board itself turn around. Follow the steps below to find out how to do this.

1. Gently pull the rig up until only the end of the boom is in the water. The board will slowly move round until the sail lies on the leeward side.

2. Continue to pull the rig out of the water and get into the secure position as before.

Turning around on the spot

When you first get the feel of windsurfing it is easy to get over-enthusiastic and end up far away from where you started, unable to get back. You can avoid this predicament by first learning how to turn the board around to face the opposite direction, as shown below.

The technique

The photos below show you how to turn the nose of the board towards and then through the wind. If you turn the nose of the board away from the wind you are likely to end up a long way from your starting point. This is because, until you can perform the manoeuvre quickly and confidently, you will be blown downwind as you are turning.

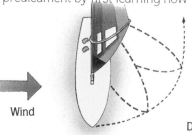

Wind

Turning the nose away from the wind: the wind can push you downwind during the turn.

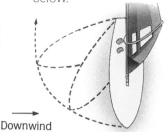

Downwind

Turning the nose through the wind: the wind is less likely to push you downwind.

Get into the secure position, then gently lean the mast towards the back of the board. The front of the board will gradually turn towards the wind.

Keeping the rig directly in front of you, and your back to the wind, shuffle around the front of the board. Your feet should stay close to the mast foot.

After the nose of the board has passed through the wind, incline the rig towards the front of the board in order to complete the 180° turn.

At the completion of the turn, you should be back in the secure position with your feet equally spaced either side of the mast foot.

Problem box

Problem You cannot control the sail and keep falling off.

Solution There are a number of things you could be doing wrong:

1. The steps you are taking around the mast foot are too large.

2. The movement of the sail is not relaxed enough – it should be a smooth motion.

3. You are looking down at your feet as you move around the mast foot. Try to avoid doing this, as it stops you from watching the sail's movements.

4. Your feet and body are not in a "V" position with the rig as you move around the board.

Improving your technique

You can speed up the turn by moving the mast back further and more quickly. Move your back foot further back for greater leverage, and remove your front hand from the mast to enable you to bring the rig further back.

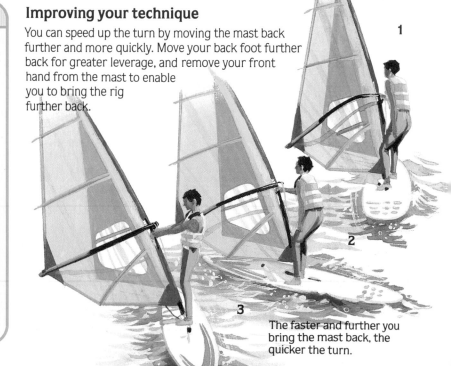

The faster and further you bring the mast back, the quicker the turn.

Moving off

Now that you have learnt how to turn around, it is time to learn one of the most exciting lessons in windsurfing: how to start moving. The basic steps are shown below: you can find out how to steer on pages 12-13, along with tips on improving your technique. First get into the secure position (see page 9) with your back to the wind and the board facing the direction you aim to go in. Look beyond the nose of the board and select a point to head towards. This is important because at this stage you want to sail directly across the wind, not towards or away from it. This course is known as a beam reach.

Take your back hand* off the mast. Move your back foot further back over the daggerboard case, still over the centreline.

Move your front foot back behind the mast. It should be parallel with the centreline of the board and pointing forwards.

Turn to face your goal and pull the mast towards the wind, until the rig begins to feel lighter (the balance point).

Without stretching, place your back hand on the boom and use it to pull the sail in very gently until it is just full of wind.**

As you move off, place your front hand on the boom, transfer your weight on to your back foot, and lean back.

To slow down, ease out with your back hand. To stop, transfer your hands on to the mast and return to the secure position.

How it works: the wind in the sail

1

Fast airflow causing low pressure area.

Slow airflow causing high pressure area.

Wind

As the wind hits the sail, it is divided into two airflows. The airflow on the windward side of the sail is slowed by the curved shape of the sail. The resulting build-up of air forms an area of high pressure. On the leeward side, the shape of the sail increases the speed of the airflow forming an area of low pressure.

2

Board shoots forward to escape pressure.

Low pressure area sucks sail towards it.

Wind

The wind in the high pressure area is sucked towards the area of low pressure, and pushes the sail with it. The board is prevented from moving sideways with the sail by the combined resistance of the daggerboard, board and your body. The resulting build-up of pressure forces the board to shoot forwards.

3

Turbulent leeward flow caused by sail not sheeted in enough.

Turbulent windward flow caused by oversheeting.

When the wind passes smoothly over both sides of the sail, it is known as laminar flow. If the sail angle to the wind is not just right, turbulent airflow will develop, and slow the board down.

*Your back hand is the hand nearest the back of the board.
**This is known as sheeting in.

Sailing technique

Most people spend a lot of time falling into the water when they first try to move off. This can be very tiring, especially since you have to pull the rig out of the water again each time.

Below there are tips on how to avoid falling in, as well as advice on improving your technique.

Perfecting your stance

The correct stance varies according to the strength of the wind as shown here.

Both arms straight (though if you feel you are losing control, slightly bend your front arm).

Use your body-weight to control the power of the sail, rather than stretching already tensed muscles.

More weight on your back foot. Body leaning out slightly to counterbalance the force on the sail.

Hands and feet positioned further back along the boom and board.

Force 3

Forces 1 and 2

Mast vertical

Arm slightly bent at elbow.

Hands approximately shoulder-width apart.

Body straight, leaning back very slightly.

Rear leg bent at the knee and relaxed.

Weight evenly balanced between front and back foot.

Back foot over daggerboard case.

Front leg held rigid to help transfer power from the sail into the board.

Front foot directly behind mast.

The overhand grip: palms are placed over the top of the boom.

The combined grip: front palm under the boom, back palm over it.

Many people find that it is most comfortable if they hold the boom with an overhand grip. A popular alternative is the combined grip, where the front hand grips the boom from underneath, and the back hand grips it from the top. You should use whichever you find most comfortable.

Problem box

If you find you are falling off a lot, run through the list of common mistakes below and try to work out what you are doing wrong. Then try to put it right on your next attempt.

★ Your body is too rigid. Try relaxing, keeping your arms and legs slightly bent.
★ You are not keeping your body-weight over the centreline of the board. In light winds, this is just as important as when balancing on the board without the rig. It is only when the wind reaches Force 3 that you need to lean out to counterbalance the power in the sail.
★ Your movements are too rushed and exaggerated. Try to make relaxed, gentle movements as you prepare to move off.

Emergency procedure

If you feel you are about to fall backwards, pull in the sail with your back hand and quickly bend your knees to bring your body-weight over the centre of the board.

To avoid falling forwards, ease out with your back hand to reduce the power in the sail. Alternatively, let go with first the back and then the front hand, and return to the secure position.

Steering on the move

When moving, you steer in the same way as when in the secure position.* If the wind is very light, the mast movements must be emphasized to have any effect. Get the feel of the movements by sailing an 'S' shaped course (see below). Ensure that the sail is sheeted in correctly after each turn by allowing the sail to flap slightly, then pulling it in until it is still.

To turn towards the wind, lean the rig towards the back of the board by extending your back arm. Transfer your weight on to your back foot.

To bear away from the wind, draw the rig across your body by extending your front arm. Transfer your weight on to your front foot.

How it works: steering

On page 11 you saw that the forward movement of the board across the wind is caused by the air pressure on the sail working against the resistance of the daggerboard, your body and the board.

The area on the sail where the pressure is greatest is the centre of effort (CE). The greatest resistance on the board is known as the centre of lateral resistance (CLR).

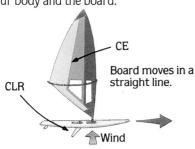

CE

CLR

Board moves in a straight line.

Wind

CE

CLR

Board bears away from the wind.

Wind

CE

CLR

Board turns into the wind.

Wind

In order for the board to move forwards in a straight line, the CE needs to be directly in line with the CLR, as shown in the diagram above.

With the sail leaning forward, the CE moves ahead of the CLR. The result is as if you had pushed the front of the board; it bears away from the wind.

If you tilt the sail back, the CE moves behind the CLR. The board then moves into the wind. The further you pull it back, the greater the effect.

*See page 9.

Sailing upwind

When you were learning how to sail on a beam reach, you may have found that the wind blew you downwind from your starting point and it took you some time to travel back upwind. Below you can find out how to sail an efficient upwind course without needing to use the services of a rescue boat.

Upwind courses

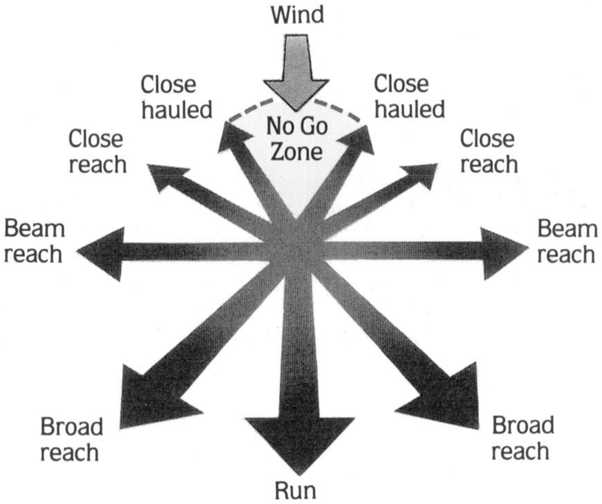

The diagram on the right shows all the courses that a windsurfer can sail. As you can see, this is in every direction apart from an area of almost 45° either side of the wind direction. This area is called the No Go Zone. If you try to sail in the No Go Zone, the board will either stop or be blown backwards.

So far you have learnt how to sail on a beam reach and to steer so that you can change course to either sail closer to the wind (a close reach) or further away from it (a broad reach). However, to make much headway upwind, you must sail on a close-hauled course. The photos below show you how to manoeuvre the board so that you are sailing close hauled.

Wind

Close hauled · Close hauled
No Go Zone
Close reach · Close reach
Beam reach · Beam reach
Broad reach · Broad reach
Run

The close-hauled course

Sail on a beam reach, then turn upwind on to a close reach by selecting a new goal point and leaning the rig towards the back of the board.

When you are pointing towards your new goal point, return the rig to the sailing position, easing in slightly. You are now sailing on a close reach.

By repeating the process described on the left you should be able to sail a course on the edge of the No Go Zone. This is the close-hauled course.

Problem box

It is easy to sail into the No Go Zone. Here are the warning signals:
1. The sail fills with wind on the wrong side.
2. The sail is over the centreline of the board.
3. The board slows down, then stops.
Unless you act quickly, you will fall in. Bear away by leaning the mast forwards.

Sailing an upwind course

Because it is impossible to sail directly into the wind, it is necessary to sail a zig-zag course to reach a point which is directly upwind. You do this by turning the board through the wind, as shown in the diagram on the right.

On page 10 you found out how to turn the board, starting from the secure position, but to have to return to the secure position every time you wanted to turn around would be slow and inefficient. Instead, follow the steps outlined on the opposite page to learn how to turn the board through the wind without stopping. This is known as tacking.

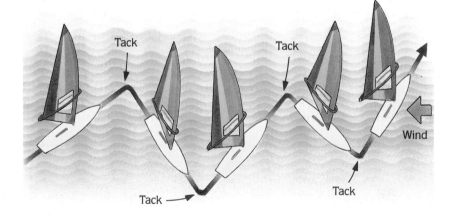

Tack

Tack

Tack

Tack

Wind

To avoid losing ground, try to tack quickly and get underway again as soon as possible.

Between tacks it is very important to sail on a close-hauled course; it is tempting to bear away from the wind a little to go faster, but you will not make as much progress upwind.

14

How to tack

Sailing close hauled, move your front hand from the boom to the mast. Then move your front foot across the centreline of the board, just in front of the mast foot. Lean the rig to the back of the board.

The board will swiftly turn towards the wind. Just before it is facing directly into the wind, transfer your back hand on to the mast. Quickly move your feet forward, side by side in front of the mast.

Now lean the rig towards the front of the board until the board is positioned at right angles to the wind. Move into the secure position before sailing off and steering on to a new close-hauled course.

Problem box

If you stay on the wrong side of the board for too long, you will fall in. Instead, try to move quickly and confidently as soon as the board starts to turn through the wind.

Once you have mastered the art of tacking, you will find it quicker to resume the sailing position straight after the tack, rather than returning to the secure position first.

More advanced tacks

Below are two progressions of the basic tack. Both these tacks involve sailing the board on to its new course before jumping around the mast.

When performed well, the boom to boom tack is quicker than both the basic and extended tacks since you do not handle the mast at all. However, it can take some time to master and you may find yourself falling in the water a good deal.

Extended tack

Lean the rig towards the back of the board, put your front hand on the mast and your front foot in front of the mast, as with the basic tack.

This time, when the board has turned so that it is directly facing the wind, stay where you are and keep the sail over the back of the board.

Push the tail of the board further under the rig with your back foot. At this point, the board will stop moving forward and may start to reverse.

Just as the board stops, step quickly around the mast, replacing your front hand on the mast with your back hand. Place your free hand on the boom, and sheet in.

Boom to boom tack

Move your front foot in front of the mast, leaning the rig to the back of the board and keeping both hands on the boom.

Sail the board through the wind and on to its new course, pushing the tail with your feet, as for the extended tack.

Remove your back hand from the boom and take it over your front arm, around the mast and on to the other side of the boom.

Step quickly around the rig, transferring your old front hand on to the other side of the boom. Now sheet in.

Sailing downwind

You now know how to sail upwind (on a close haul), across the wind (on a beam reach), and slightly away from the wind (on a broad reach or close reach). The photos below show you how to sail with the wind directly behind you, the board and your sail. This is called a run.

You might think that you would be able to go faster on a run than on any other course because the wind is pushing you along from behind. However, there is no suction from the leeward side as there is on other courses (see page 11), so in fact it is not as fast as sailing on a reach.

Sailing on a run

Sailing on a beam reach, lean the sail forwards by extending your front arm. The board will turn on to a broad reach course.

Keeping the mast forwards, ease the sail out gently with your back hand, and then pull it in slowly with your front hand.

Now move both your feet so that they are positioned either side of the centreline of the board, pointing forwards.

Move the rig across your body so that the sail is at right angles to the board. You are now sailing on a run.

Steering

Slowing down

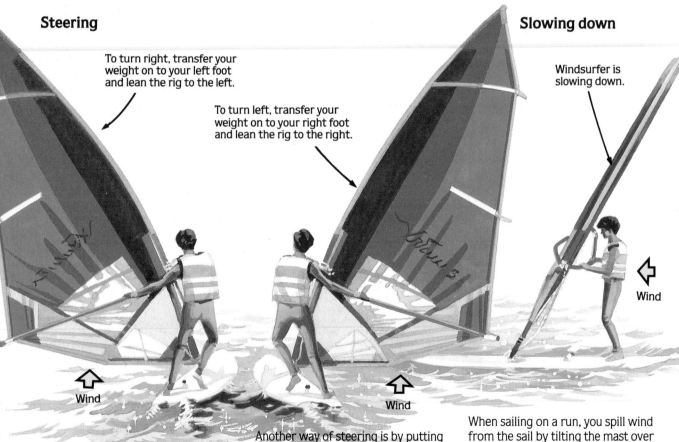

To turn right, transfer your weight on to your left foot and lean the rig to the left.

To turn left, transfer your weight on to your right foot and lean the rig to the right.

Windsurfer is slowing down.

Wind

Wind

Wind

You can steer the board on a run by leaning the rig to the right or left.

Another way of steering is by putting pressure on one or other of your feet. For speed, combine both methods.

When sailing on a run, you spill wind from the sail by tilting the mast over your head. To increase speed again, bring it back to an upright position.

Gybing

When you are sailing downwind, it is much quicker to turn the back of the board through the wind rather than steering back upwind to tack. This is called gybing. Practise the gybing manoeuvre, following the instructions below.

Manoeuvre yourself and your board so that you are sailing on a run. Transfer your back hand from the boom on to the mast.

As the board begins to turn, take your front hand off the boom. Then by moving your feet, return to the secure position.*

Now move into the sailing position and sail away on a beam reach, steering by moving the rig backwards or forwards.

The flare gybe

A slightly more advanced and faster form of gybing is the flare gybe. The wind needs to be at least Force 2** before you can perform a successful flare gybe.

From a close reach, bear away from the wind by bringing the rig forwards. At the same time, lean it and your body towards the windward side of the board.

Move towards the back of the board, keeping the rig and your body weighted to the windward side. Your feet may well become submerged.

As the board begins to turn, move your hands down the boom and make gentle pulls on the sail to scoop the wind and accelerate the turn.

The board will now rotate so that the back of the sail points towards the front of the board. Quickly move back up the board to stop turning further.

Release the boom with the rear hand and take the mast. This now becomes the front hand; release the boom with the old front hand.

Bring the rig swiftly across your body, towards the wind. Place your new back hand on to the boom again. Sheet in and sail away on your new course.

How it works: the apparent wind

On every course except a run, you will find that the wind begins to shift slightly as you pick up speed, and you need to sheet in to keep maximum power in your sail. The reason for this is shown below.

Sail at slow speed

True wind | Apparent wind

Sail at medium speed

True wind | Apparent wind

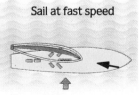

Sail at fast speed

True wind | Apparent wind

When you are standing still on land facing the wind, you will feel the wind on your face. This is called the true wind. If you turn around and start running, although the true wind is now behind you, you will still feel the wind on your face.

Likewise in windsurfing the wind is a combination of the true wind and the wind felt as the board moves through the water. This combined force is called the apparent wind. The faster you go, the more the apparent wind will be coming from in front of the board.

To position the sail at the best angle to catch the apparent wind, you will need to sheet in further.

*When you become more confident, you will be able to gybe without returning to the secure position.
**See page 58 to find out how to identify wind strengths.

Test your skills

Below are a number of exercises which will test how well you have mastered all the basic windsurfing skills covered so far, and will help to improve your technique and confidence. If possible, try them out on flat water in Force 2 or Force 3 wind.

Whenever you have completed an exercise, analyse your performance and try to work out how you could do better.

One-handed boom control

Trailing foot exercise

Foot control

1. See how small a wake you can create behind the board by varying the position of your feet. The smaller the wake, the faster you will travel.

2. Take your front foot off the board and trail it in the water for about 30 seconds. Then do the same with your back foot.

On the run

Stand back on the board so that the tail sinks in the water. See how long you can sail like this.

Kneel on the board.

Sit on the board.

Boom control

1. Move your hands together along the boom until you find a position where you can take the strain of the rig with just one hand.

2. Put your hands as far away from each other as possible on the boom.

3. Remove both hands from the boom and clap before replacing them.

One-handed gybe

Mimicking exercise

Gybing

Touch the water when you are half-way through a gybe, first with one hand, then the other.

Pumping

See if you can make the board go faster by pumping the sail. Sailing on a reach, suddenly pull the boom, towards you (picture 1), then sheet out (picture 2). Repeat this scooping action about four times in succession.

With a friend

1. Take the role of leader and sail along, varying your course and incorporating as many tricks as possible. The other person should follow behind mimicking you. Now swap roles.
2. Set off from the same point, one after the other. See who can sail closest to the wind.
3. Mark a starting and finishing line with buoys. Then race to the finishing line.

Get into reverse

See if you can manage to sail backwards on a beam reach. Sheet out until the board comes to a stop, then transfer your hands to the other side of the boom. By sheeting in, you will start to move backwards.

Sailing back to shore

You can easily damage your board and sail if you do not control your return to shore sufficiently well. Follow the instructions below for a well-executed return.

Slow down as you come towards the shore. When the water is around knee-height, stop the board by getting into the secure position.

Gently lay the rig in the water, on the leeward side of the board. Climb off the board, release the safety leash, then remove the mast foot and daggerboard.

Finally, carry the board and daggerboard back to shore as shown above. Then go back for the sail (two easy ways of carrying your sail are shown on page 57).

19

Strong wind technique

The first few attempts at sailing in strong winds can be extremely demoralizing; many people give up trying to sail in winds over Force 3 as they decide they are not strong enough. However, strength is not a major requirement for strong wind sailing. It is vital, though, to adjust your technique to cope with the winds. It is also worthwhile investing in a smaller, more manageable, sail (see pages 48-49).

Pulling up the rig

Pulling the rig up slowly and steadily would result in the wind tearing it from your hands. A quick, determined action is vital so that the rig spends as little time as possible moving from the water to the secure position.

Positioning one foot either side of the mast foot, bend your knees until you are almost crouching. Keep your back straight.

With one strong jerk, pull the whole rig out of the water. Keeping the rig partly submerged will cause the board to move off.

With one hand on the mast and one on the boom, pull the sail right across your body, then lean back, taking it with you. Now sheet in.

Strong wind stance

You need to alter your stance as shown here to cope with the extra wind. In strong winds, the board has a tendency to dip into the water at the front, and the windward edge (rail) may rise (known as railing). This slows the board down, so you need to alter your foot positions to keep it level. This is called trimming the board.

By pulling the sail down over your body, you can lessen the amount of sail area that is available to the wind, and so decrease the wind power.

Pull the mast down over your body.

Both arms straight.

Lean your body out to counteract the force of the wind in the sail.

Keep your weight low by bending at the knees and hips.

Feet positioned further back and to windward.

Gusts

A common feature of strong wind sailing is that the wind is constantly changing in strength and direction. A strong gust of wind could throw you into the water if you are not prepared for it.

A gust can easily be spotted as it creates a dark patch of small ripples on the water beneath it as it travels. If you see one coming, you can react in one of the following two ways. The first method involves depowering your sail until the gust has passed. The second method enables you to use the additional wind power to increase your speed, and is good racing technique.

Either: ease the sail out with your back hand, and bring your weight over the centre of the board. Keep the mast close to your body. Sheet in again when the gust has passed.

Or: lean right out, keeping your arms straight but dropping your bottom slightly. As soon as it has passed, bend your knees and move back over the board.

Planing

In winds over Force 3, you can achieve very fast speeds by allowing the board to skim across the surface of the water rather than plough through it. This is known as planing. For the board to start planing, it needs to be level in the water. You therefore need to trim it, as explained on the opposite page.

To check whether or not you are planing, look behind the board. A gap between the wake and the board indicates that you are planing.

Board not planing: wake is attached to the board.

Board planing: wake is detached from the board.

Retracting the daggerboard

In light winds, the daggerboard is kept down on all courses. However, in strong winds the board will go faster and be easier to manoeuvre on certain courses if the daggerboard is not completely down. For this reason, most boards are now fitted with a daggerboard which can be either partially or fully retracted.

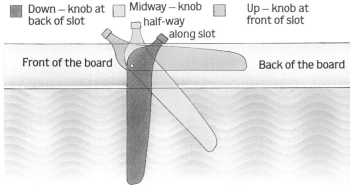

Down – knob at back of slot

Midway – knob half-way along slot

Up – knob at front of slot

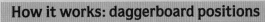

Front of the board

Back of the board

You can retract your daggerboard while still on the move by pushing the knob firmly with your back foot.

How it works: daggerboard positions

Going upwind: daggerboard down.

Going upwind in strong wind: daggerboard midway.

When sailing upwind, the wind is trying to push the board backwards and sideways, so the daggerboard normally has to be fully down to provide maximum lateral resistance.

However, when the wind is very strong, the pressure on the daggerboard may force the board to tip on its edge (rail). To reduce railing, retract the daggerboard to the midway position.

Going directly downwind: daggerboard up.

Going crosswind at high speed in rough water: daggerboard midway.

When sailing on a run, no lateral resistance is required. By retracting the daggerboard completely, you reduce drag in the water and make the board more controllable.

When on a beam or broad reach, the board can be either fully or partially retracted. The position you choose will depend on such things as your speed and the state of the water.

Using the mast track and footstraps

Most all-round boards have sliding mast tracks, enabling you to alter the position of the mast foot. They also have footstraps, which hold your feet on the board and can give you greater leverage.

Although you don't need either in light winds, in winds of Force 4 and over they can have a great effect on your speed and performance, so it is well worth learning how to use them.

How it works: the mast foot position

If you position the mast foot right at the front of the track, the weight of the rig will lower the nose of the board into the water. This is useful when sailing upwind as it combines with the daggerboard in providing extra lateral resistance (see page 13).

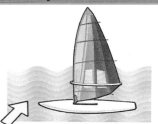

Mast foot forward: provides better upwind performance.

If you position the mast towards the back of the track, the nose of the board will rise. This causes the board to go faster downwind as there is less drag in the water, and it encourages the board to start planing in strong winds (see page 21).

Mast foot back: increases speed on downwind courses.

Using the mast track

Most mast tracks are operated by pressing on a pedal with your foot. This releases the mast foot.

Now lean forwards on the boom and push your front knee against the mast to slide it forwards.

Alternatively, pull the boom towards you in order to slide it to the back of the track.

If the track is very stiff, place your front hand on the mast, just below the boom, to help it along.

Footstraps

In strong winds, particularly in wavy sea conditions, footstraps are essential to prevent your feet from being bounced off the board. Also, by keeping your foot position constant, they give you greater control and leverage on the board. They are only of use when the board is planing (see page 21); at slower speeds, your feet will be wrongly positioned and the board will lose its balance or cause the tail of the board to sink in the water.

The number of footstraps a board has, and their positions on the board, varies widely according to the design and the manufacturer. The picture on the right shows the most common formation on an all-round board and explains when you should use them.

Expert straps* – normal position for front and back feet. Best position for strong wind gybes (see pages 28-29) and footsteering, as weight is then centred over the turning part of the board.

Training straps – for use until you feel confident enough to move back into the expert straps. For front and back feet.

Beating strap – for sailing upwind when maximum lateral resistance is needed. Can only be used when mast foot is in its forward position. For front foot only.

22   *Otherwise known as gybing straps.

Adjusting the footstraps

It is vital to make sure that you adjust the straps so they fit properly. You could easily break an ankle if they are too loose and the foot slips through or so tight that the foot becomes trapped. When fitting a strap, position your foot so that only the toes protrude, and adjust the strap so

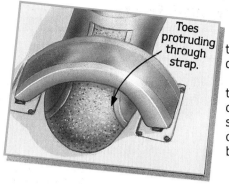

Toes protruding through strap.

that your foot feels secure but comfortable.

You can check that the strap is not too tight by bringing your other foot over to the far side of the board. You should now be able to take your foot out of the strap and step over the board.

Getting into the footstraps

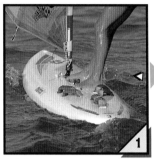 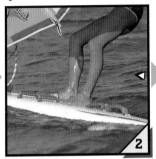  

Sail as fast as possible on a broad reach with your feet out of the straps. Make sure your daggerboard is fully retracted.

Slowly move your front foot into the front training strap, keeping your back foot free to help keep the board level in the water.

Move your back foot into the rear training strap. If the tail of the board sinks, bring your back foot forward again to regain speed.

Carry out the same smooth movements to get into the expert straps. Remember, you will need to be travelling very fast.

Sailing upwind

When sailing upwind, do not put your back foot into either strap. Instead, keep it free to help you keep your balance and stop the board from flipping over on its rail (see page 20).

Footsteering

When planing crosswind or downwind with the daggerboard retracted, you can steer the board by weighting either side of it. When sailing upwind, the daggerboard is still down and so you have to steer in the normal way. Test your skills by sailing a curved course as shown below, using your weight to turn the board.

Wind

To turn into the wind, push down on the windward edge of the board with your heels.

To bear away from the wind, bend your knees and lean your body towards the leeward side.

(see page 20).

Checklist

Here is a summary of strong wind positions for the daggerboard and mast foot.

UPWIND

Daggerboard: down

Mast foot: front

CROSSWIND

Daggerboard: midway

Mast foot: middle/back

DOWNWIND

Daggerboard: up

Mast foot: front/middle

Wearing a harness

Sailing in strong winds can be very tiring on the arms. A harness takes the strain off your arms, transferring the load on to your legs and back. You then only need to use your arms to make fine adjustments to the positioning of the sail.

Types of harness

There are three main types of harness; the chest harness, waist harness and seat harness (also known as a nappy harness).

Chest harness

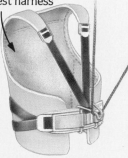

The chest harness is easy to use, has some buoyancy, and has a high hook which is easier to unhook from in a hurry. However, it gives little support to the lower back.

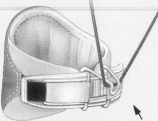

Waist harness

The waist harness is a very simple form of harness. It is very light and allows total freedom of movement. However, it does tend to slip upwards.

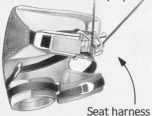

Seat harness

The seat harness is more difficult to use at first, but is the most efficient type of harness. Most of the load is carried by the legs, and your lower back is well supported. It allows you to use all of your body-weight to control the rig.

Buying a harness

When choosing a harness, make sure it fits well and is comfortable. If possible, test it out before buying. Shops often have ropes hanging from the ceiling which you can hook into. Whichever type of harness you choose, make sure it includes all the following features.

★ Low back to support the lumbar area of your back.

★ Sliding spreader bar: this spreads the load. Look for one which is at least 25cm long.

★ V-shaped safety hook to minimise possibility of harness lines getting tangled around the hook.

★ Quick-release system for use in emergencies.

★ Stiff harness lines (thin nylon rope covered in plastic tubing). These eliminate any slim chance of the lines becoming entangled.

★ As much buoyancy as possible.

Setting up the harness lines

Correct positioning of your harness lines on the boom is absolutely vital. If they are badly positioned, your balance will be wrong and you will find it difficult to control the rig.

Stand the rig up in a sheltered place, resting the mast foot against your foot. Position yourself and the rig as if you were sailing on a beam reach.

Let go with your back hand then slide your front hand down the boom until you find the position where the rig is balanced (the balance point).

Land practice

It is a good idea to practise using your harness on land before venturing into the water. You will then feel confident enough to hook and unhook without looking down to ensure that the hook and rope have connected.

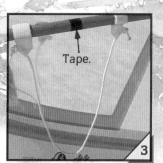

With your back to the wind, stand and face the sail. Place your hands just outside of the harness line.

Now flick the line towards your hook by jerking the boom towards you, at the same time moving your hips forward so that the hook goes over the line.

Lean back until your arms are almost fully extended. The harness should now take your weight. If not, your lines are too long, so adjust them.

Once you are used to the feeling of leaning right back, unhook from the line. To do this, pull the boom towards you until the line drops out of the hook.

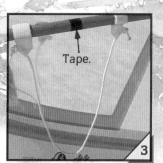

Tape.

Mark the balance point. Now firmly attach the harness lines either side of this mark. Most lines have velcro straps for this purpose.

Check the position by hooking in and releasing both hands. You should be able to take the weight of the rig without it trying to fall away.

Now adjust the length of the lines. For maximum comfort, you should almost be able to stretch your arms out when hooked into the harness.

When to use the harness

Before using a harness, you must be able to sail in at least Force 4 winds.* Should the harness lines break, you will need to be able to sail home again. Do not use a harness when sailing on a run, as you will find it difficult to spot oncoming gusts.**

Always unhook before changing direction or coming to a halt, otherwise you could find yourself being catapulted right over the sail.

*See page 58 to find out how to identify wind strengths.
**See page 21 for more about spotting and coping with gusts.

The beach start and water start

The beach start and water start are ways of setting sail without first having to haul the rig out of the water.

Mastering these techniques will make windsurfing in stronger winds easier and more fun.

The beach start

A beach start involves getting on to your board from shallow water. This is less tiring than uphauling and also makes it easier to avoid waves breaking directly on to the shore. To practise the beach start you need a shallow, sloping beach which has a cross-shore wind. You can use any type of board which has a retractable daggerboard.

Once you are proficient, you can try a beach start on a short board without a daggerboard (see page 47). For now, have your daggerboard fully retracted.

Connect the board and rig. Position the board so that it points out to sea, with the mast pointing behind it.

Stand to windward of the board and pull the rig up, holding the mast above the boom with your front hand.

Lift the board by the rail or a footstrap with your back hand and push it into knee-deep water.

Place your back hand on the boom and position the board on a close reach by pushing it with your foot.*

Put your back foot on the centreline and your front hand on the boom, close to the mast, ready to sail.

Straighten your arms, pushing the boom above you so that the rig moves upright and fills with wind.

Now pull your front foot up on to the board, close to the mast foot, as you start to move off.

Quickly switch your weight to your front foot and lean the mast forwards in order to bear away from the wind.

Problem box

Problem You have difficulty sailing away from the shore.

Solution When you straighten your arms, extend them as high as possible, allowing the rig to fill with wind and thus supply as much power as possible to the board.

Problem You cannot get close enough to the board to put your foot on it.

Solution Either make sure you are approaching the board from the side rather than from the rear, or check that you are lifting the boom high enough above you.

Problem Your board turns into the wind as soon as any weight is put upon it.

Solution Ensure that your back foot is on the centreline of the board, and also that you are putting plenty of pressure on your front foot and on the mast foot.

*Another way of manoeuvring the board is to push down on the mast (board points away from you) or pull on it (turns towards you).

The water start

The water start is a way of getting back on to the board from deep water, using the wind to help you. Like the beach start, it saves you from wasting energy in pulling the sail up out of the water.

If you want to sail on a short board in fairly strong winds, it is essential to master the water start, as it is very difficult to uphaul on a short board. Ideal conditions for a water start are Force 4 or 5.

In chest-high water, position your board pointing into the wind, with the rig at 90° to it and the clew downwind, as shown above.

Get in front of the mast, just above the boom. Place your front hand on the mast, using your other arm to help you swim upwind.

Push the mast upwards to enable more wind to get under the sail. Now position yourself directly under the sail.

Keeping the mast at right angles to the wind, place both hands on the boom, and use it to push the sail further up.

The front of the board will now bear away from the wind. As it does so, place your back foot on the board, over the centreline.

Extend your arms to raise the rig as high as you can. Push down on your back foot and kick hard with your front foot.

Stand up on your back leg and use the wind to help bring your front leg on to the board, again over the centreline.

Quickly move your feet forward on the board and get into the normal sailing position, bearing away from the wind as you do so.

Problem box

Because the water start is a very similar manoeuvre to the beach start, many of the problems associated with the start also apply to the water start. Check the problem box on the previous page.

Problem The boom catches in the water just as you are about to start moving.

Solution Tug the mast sharply into the wind.

Rig recovery

You may find that the rig is lying on the wrong side of the board for the direction you wish to sail in (see right). The least tiring solution is to sail off on the opposite tack, then turn around. However, this may be impossible if there is an obstacle in your way and you may have to swim the rig around to the other side. Another problem may be that the clew points upwind. If so, you need to flip the sail in the following way:

1. Hold the rear of the board with your front hand. With your back hand, lift the boom end until the wind gets under the sail.

2. As the wind catches the sail, let go of the boom and allow the sail to flip over into the correct downwind position.

To sail off on port*, the rig must lie to the left of the board.

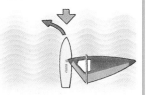

To sail off on starboard*, the rig must lie to the right of the board.

*See page 59 for an easy way of identifying port and starboard.

27

Strong wind gybes

On page 23, you found out how to steer the board with your feet rather than by moving the rig. In high winds, you can go further than that; you can gybe using your feet to execute the turn, only moving the rig to the other side of the board towards the end of the manoeuvre. These gybes can only be achieved when you are travelling at top speed in winds of at least Force 4.

Practise the carve gybe, duck gybe and slam gybe in flat water, with your daggerboard fully retracted. Always check behind you before starting a gybe to avoid hitting anything.

The carve gybe

Plane on a reach using the expert straps. Unhook your harness and bear slightly away from the wind. Now move to a more upright position with your weight over the centreline.

Take your back foot out of its strap and press down on the leeward rail with it. As you turn, push both knees towards the leeward rail. Your upper body should be upright.

The duck gybe

Start the duck gybe following the first two steps of the carve gybe. Now slide your back hand towards the back of the boom.

Carve gybe

Sail flips around the front of the board.

Board turns on the inside rail.

Board turns on the inside rail.

Duck gybe

Sail flips over the middle of the board.

Sail flips around the front of the board.

Slam gybe

Board pivots round on the tail in a tight circle.

Continue to hold the rig upright as the board turns away from the wind and on to its new broad reach course. You will notice a lot of pressure on your back hand.

As the pressure increases, transfer your back hand to the mast and remove your front foot from its strap. Keep the mast close to you as the sail flips around the front of the board.

Keeping hold of the mast with your back hand, release the boom with your old front hand. Pull the rig forwards and to windward, then sheet in with your new back hand.

As you move off, transfer your front hand to the boom, preparing for a sudden pull in the sail by crouching down. Once you have regained speed, get back into the straps.

Let go of the boom with your front hand. As the rig starts to swing over your head, cross your front hand over your back hand.

Now take your back hand off the boom, and use your front hand to push the rig firmly to the outside of the turn.

Take hold of the other side of the boom with the back hand. Transfer your old front hand on to the other side of the boom.

Sheet in and steer on to your new course. Finally, move your front foot then your back foot across the board and into the straps.

The slam gybe

Follow the first two steps of the carve gybe sequence. Now slow the board down by letting the sail out with your back hand.

Keeping your front foot straight, bend your back leg and transfer all your weight on to it. The board should pivot around the tail.

During the turning of the board, you will be sailing clew first. Now let the sail swing around the front of the board, and sheet in.

To stop the board from turning too far into the wind quickly move forwards along the board and sheet in tightly.

Basic freestyle

Freestyle means doing tricks on your board. On these two pages you will find some basic tricks which can be picked up fairly easily with practice. On the following pages the techniques progress in difficulty, finishing with some really spectacular stunts.

The degree of difficulty of each trick is shown by the number of stars next to it. One star denotes an easy trick, ten stars a difficult one. Most techniques come somewhere in the middle.

Equipment

The best type of board to use for freestyle is a flat one with wide, deep rails and a lot of volume (see page 46). Durability is important to avoid damage to the board, but its surface should not be abrasive, as you can easily scrape your feet and ankles when practising freestyle stunts. A polyethylene board is ideal, being both tough and fairly smooth (see page 47).

Your rig should be a light one with a fairly short boom for manoeuvrability (see page 48). A semi-battened sail is best for easy handling, but a fully battened one would do.

Clothing

Always wear a wetsuit when first learning to freestyle, as it will protect your shins. If you still feel vulnerable, you could buy some shin pads. Do not wear a harness as it will inhibit your movement, and remove the lines from your boom.

Weather conditions

For most freestyle techniques, the ideal conditions are a Force 2-3 wind, and calm water. Some tricks, such as the head dip, require a stronger breeze. Where they differ from the general rule, optimum weather conditions are specified in the instructions for a technique.

Both arms slightly bent and relaxed.

The clew is over the front of the board.

Mast leans back slightly.

To return to normal: continue with a basic gybe (see page 17).

Sailing back to front ★ ★

This technique involves turning around on your board so that you are standing on the windward side of the board with your back to the sail.

1. Pointing the board across the wind, sheet out until the sail starts to flap.

2. Move your back hand close to the front end of the boom. Release your front hand. Turn your body to face the wind.

3. Pull the mast slightly to windward and move what was your front hand behind you, on to the middle of the boom.

4. Place your new front hand on the mast, and sail along with both arms stretched out behind you your body leaning out.

Clew-first sailing ★ ★

The idea of this technique is to point the back end of the sail towards the front end of the board.

1. Whilst sailing along on a broad reach, lean the rig towards the front of the board and replace your back hand with your front hand on the back end of the boom.

2. As the mast swings to point directly away from you, grab the other side of the boom, close to the mast, with your back hand.

3. Let go of the boom with your front hand and move it round to the other side, sliding both hands along the boom until they are positioned as for normal sailing. You are now sailing clew first.

Back hand controls the sheeting of the sail.

Front hand keeps the mast steady.

Back foot is slightly bent for greater control.

To return to normal: simply perform the manoeuvre in reverse.

Lying on your board ★ ★ ★

This trick consists of manoeuvring yourself into a reclining position on your board, while you are sailing along.

1. While sailing on a run and keeping your hands in the normal position, sit astride your board.

2. Keep sailing on a straight course downwind. Now pull your legs out of the water and sit on the board with your knees slightly bent.

The head dip ★ ★ ★

The head dip requires you to lean back and dip the crown of your head in the water whilst sailing along. You need a fairly strong breeze (at least Force 3) to do a head dip from a standing position as here; in light winds it is easier to sit on the board first.

1. While sailing on a close reach, lean backwards and outwards, arching your back as much as you can.

The pirouette ★ ★ ★

This involves spinning through 360° on the ball of your foot. Before trying a pirouette, practise the first two stage.

1. Sail on a beam reach in calm water. Sheet out until the sail flaps a little.

2. Tilt the mast to windward, then push it away from you with your front hand and let go of the boom with your back hand. Wait until the sail seems about to fall, then catch hold of the mast and

Back hand supports the sail.

Front hand supports the mast.

Arms straight.

Tuck your arms into your body.

Pivot on your foot.

3. Still holding on to the boom with your arms fully extended so that the sail continues to fill, lean back until you are lying on the board. You may find it easier to control the rig if you put one hand on the mast, and support the sail with the other hand.

To return to normal: sit up and put your legs back in the water. Replace both hands on the boom, step up on to the board, one foot at a time, and stand up.

2. Slide your feet across to the leeward side of the board. Now bend your knees, straighten your arms and arch your back as much as possible. If you are fairly supple, you should now be able to dip the crown of your head in the water.

To return to normal: once your head touches the water, pull yourself back up again by moving your feet back to their usual position, pulling hard on the boom with your hands and straightening your legs to stand up.

boom again.
When you can do this manoeuvre confidently, you can combine it with a pirouette as follows:

3. This time, the moment you let go of the mast, spin round clockwise through 360° on the ball and toes of your back foot.

4. As you complete the turn, grab the boom with both hands. Now resume the normal sailing position.

31

Railriding

Once you have mastered some of the basic freestyle techniques on the previous two pages, you may feel confident (and competent) enough to try something more sophisticated.

Below you can find out how to do a popular and very exhilarating manoeuvre known as the railride. On the opposite page, there are three variations on this basic technique.

The railride ★ ★ ★

The railride is so-called because you tilt your board on to its side in the water and ride along standing on the rail instead of the deck. You can easily bark your shins when learning this technique, so it is a good idea to wear a full-length wetsuit until you have mastered it. Push your daggerboard right down and make sure the mast foot is secure before you start.

Ideal conditions are a Force 3 wind and calm water.

To return to normal: move your front foot back on to the daggerboard and push down. As the board flips back into the normal sailing position, move first your back foot, then your front foot on to the deck. You need to make this manoeuvre quite swiftly in order to keep your balance and continue sailing a straight course.

When you have mastered the railride and can do it proficiently as shown on the right, you can learn how to combine it with other basic freestyle techniques. Some of the most popular manoeuvres are shown on the opposite page.

1. Whilst sailing along on a close reach, move your back foot towards the leeward side of the board. Transfer your weight on to it and lean back slightly.

2. Squat down, slip your front foot under the windward rail and practise tilting the board upwards. Tilt it a little further each time you try.

3. Now tilt the windward rail right up to the mast, moving your front foot on to the daggerboard and resting the thigh of your back leg on the rail.

4. Whilst maintaining as much power as possible in the sail, take your body-weight on the front foot and move your back foot on to the rail.

5. When you feel confident in this position, move your front foot on to the rail. Keep your knees bent and your body-weight low. You are now railriding.

Tail-first on the rail★ ★ ★ ★

This manoeuvre is relatively simple once you have mastered the railride, and it is great fun to learn.

1. From the normal sailing position step around the mast, keeping the rig still so that the board does not turn around. You will now be ready to sail with the back of the board positioned in front of you.

2. As the board begins to move off, tip the board on to the rail as for the normal railride.

Back of the board

3. The board will immediately try to head into the wind, so lean the mast forwards to stop this.

To return to normal: first follow the steps on the opposite page to get out of the railride. Now step around the front of the mast, again making sure that the board does not turn. Finally, resume the normal sailing position with the tail of the board behind you once more.

Clew-first sailing on the rail ★ ★ ★ ★ ★ ★

Clew-first sailing on the rail combines the clew-first manoeuvre on page 30 with the railride (see opposite). Do not attempt the railride part of the trick until you are sailing along confidently in a clew-first position.

1. From a clew-first sailing position, point the clew slightly downwards. This will help you to keep your balance for the next part of the manoeuvre.

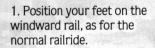

Clew is over the front of the board.

Keep your body low.

2. Now position yourself on the rail, keeping your knees bent and your body-weight low as for the normal railride.

To return to normal: first flip the board back on to the flat, then perform a basic gybe (see page 17) to return to a normal sailing stance.

Head dip on the rail ★ ★ ★ ★ ★ ★

A head dip on the rail combines the normal head dip (see page 31) with the railride in a technique which requires balance, suppleness and nerve.
   The stretch required to touch your head in the water from the rail is even greater than that needed for the normal head dip. Keep practising if you do not manage it the first time.

1. Position your feet on the windward rail, as for the normal railride.

2. Bend your knees and arch your back as much as possible, as for the normal head dip.

3. Extend your arms fully to keep the rig upright.

To return to normal: Pull hard on the boom and straighten your legs to stand on the rail. Then follow the previous instructions to get out of the railride.

33

Advanced freestyle

Once you have mastered some of the techniques shown on the previous four pages, your freestyle repertoire should be quite varied. Here you will find three of the most impressive freestyle manoeuvres you can perform: the somersault through the boom, the body drag and the duckspin tack. The latter is best learnt by trying the duck tack and spin tack separately, before attempting the complete technique.

Somersault through the boom ★ ★ ★ ★ ★ ★ ★ ★ ★

This technique is very impressive, but difficult to master. It is important to do the somersault as quickly as possible, and tuck your head in so that you do not hit it on the board.

1. Sail slowly on a beam reach. Turn to face the boom and alter the position of your hands on it so that the rest of your body can comfortably fit between them.

2. Keeping the sail as upright as possible, do a somersault through the boom, tucking your feet in close to your bottom.

3. Try to land with both feet on the board, and resume the sailing position straight away.

A loose grip on the boom

Head tucked in

Arms bent

Keep your body close to the boom for maximum control.

Body drag ★ ★ ★ ★ ★

The body drag is a good way to cool off in hot weather. It involves stepping off the board and gliding on the water for a few seconds, before returning to normal sailing. A Force 5 wind is best for this technique.

1. Sail as fast as you can on a beam reach. If you are in footstraps, step out of them.

2. Step off the board with your front foot, pointing your toes so they skim across the surface of the water.

3. Your foot will immediately be dragged towards the back of the board. As this happens, bend your back leg and lean on the rig with your front hand and on the water with your front foot.

4. Once you feel well supported, step off the board with your back foot. Let your feet glide along the surface of the water for a few seconds.

5. Meanwhile, sheet in with your back hand to keep control of the rig.

To return to normal: Once you feel yourself beginning to sink, turn your body so that your weight shifts on to your front leg. Lift your back leg out of the water and on to the board. Pull on the boom with your hands, lift your front foot on to the board and resume the usual sailing position.

Duck tack ★ ★ ★ ★

A duck tack involves tacking by ducking under the sail, rather than walking around the mast in the usual way.

Ideal conditions for a duck tack (as for a spin tack and duckspin tack) are a Force 2 wind and flat water.

1. Whilst sailing across the wind, lean the rig back until the front of the board passes through the wind.

2. Cross your front hand over your back hand, to the rear of the boom. Throw the rig forwards and upwards with your back hand.

Mast leans forward.

3. Duck underneath the sail and grab the boom close to the mast with your front hand (this was formerly your back hand). Now place your new back hand on the boom.

4. Adopt a normal sailing stance on the other side of the board. Now lean the mast forwards to steer the board on to its new course and sail off on the other tack.

Spin tack ★ ★ ★ ★ ★ ★ ★

The spin tack involves spinning through 360° whilst moving around the front of the board, as for a normal tack.

1. Sail on a close reach. Lean the mast back and grasp it with your front hand, below the boom. Hold the boom with your back hand until you are ready to spin.

2. As the board passes through the eye of the wind, release your back hand and turn your back foot towards the front of the board.

Spin around on this foot.

3. Move your front foot to the front of the mast and release the mast with your front hand. Grasp it again with your back hand, as you continue spinning.

4. Spin on your front foot, taking hold of the boom with your front hand (formerly your back hand).

5. When you are safely round the other side of the boom, take up the normal sailing position and sail the board off on its new tack.

Duckspin tack ★ ★ ★ ★ ★ ★
★ ★ ★ ★

The duckspin tack involves ducking under the sail and spinning through 360° whilst tacking. The duck tack, spin tack and pirouette are all good practice for this spectacular manoeuvre. You may find it helpful to try the duck and spin on dry land with just the rig, before attempting them in the water.

1. Sail the board into the wind and tilt the mast back so that the board turns through the wind.

2. Move your back hand back along the boom and start to turn your body away from the sail so that your back is towards the rig.

3. Let go with your back hand, throw the rig into the wind, grab the back of the boom and tug it sharply towards you. As the sail moves round, spin through 360° underneath the rig.

4. As you complete the spin, check your body with your back foot, grab the boom again on the other side with your back hand (formerly your front hand) and resume a normal sailing stance, ready to move off on the other tack.

Sailing in waves

One of the most exhilarating aspects of windsurfing is learning how to negotiate waves. This is known as wavesailing. To enjoy it, you need to have mastered strong wind gybes (see pages 28-29) as well as the beach start and water start (see pages 26-27). Below, a complete wavesailing programme takes you out to sea and back again in choppy water, teaching you all the main techniques on the way.

On pages 38-39 you can find out how to build on these techniques, trying out more advanced wavesailing tricks and jumping big waves.

Equipment

Although there are boards and rigs designed specifically for wavesailing (see pages 46-49), you can attempt all the techniques shown here using any board with a retractable daggerboard and a semi-battened sail. For the advanced techniques shown on the next two pages, you will need specialist equipment.

To make an all-round board safer for wavesailing, sand down any sharp edges such as the nose and skeg. Always wear a wetsuit at first as it gives protection if you fall off and are hit by your board.

Conditions

Ideal conditions are a sandy beach and a moderate cross-shore wind.

Should you run into problems, choppy waves can hamper attempts to rescue you, so it is especially important to observe the safety precautions outlined on page 7. Avoid hazards such as rocks, strong tides and currents, and familiarize yourself with the right of way rules concerning wavesailing (see page 59).

Parts of a wave

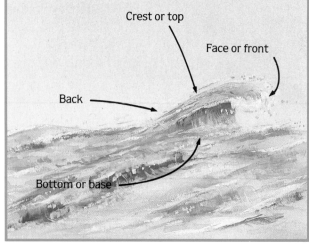

Crest or top

Face or front

Back

Bottom or base

Wavesailing routine

Launching

1

2

Before you begin, study the sequence of waves until you know when to expect the smallest ones. These will be easier to launch through.

The smallest waves often occur just after the biggest wave in the sequence has broken.

Stand in the shallows, on the windward side of the board. Hold it clear of the water. When you are ready to go, drop your board on its base and execute a beach start (see page 26).

Landing safely

10

9

Once you are in the shallows, step out of the footstraps. Climb off the board when the water is about knee-deep, supporting the mast below the boom to stop it from falling in the water. Take hold of the back footstrap, lift up your board and rig and walk on to dry land.

As you approach the shore, unhook from the harness and slow down by turning slightly into the wind and falling off the back of the waves or by depowering the sail.

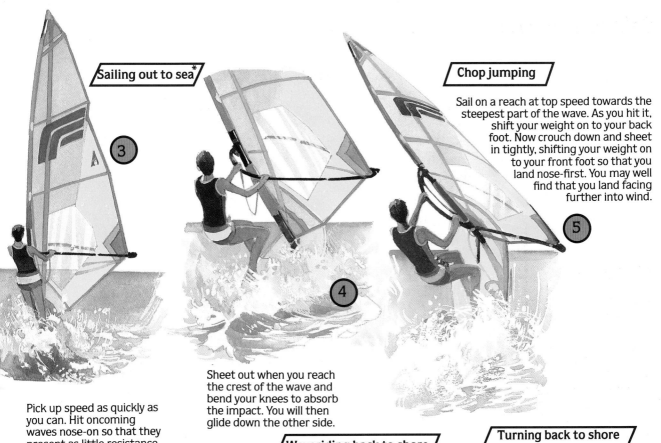

Sailing out to sea*

③

④

Pick up speed as quickly as you can. Hit oncoming waves nose-on so that they present as little resistance as possible.

Sheet out when you reach the crest of the wave and bend your knees to absorb the impact. You will then glide down the other side.

Chop jumping

Sail on a reach at top speed towards the steepest part of the wave. As you hit it, shift your weight on to your back foot. Now crouch down and sheet in tightly, shifting your weight on to your front foot so that you land nose-first. You may well find that you land facing further into wind.

⑤

Waveriding back to shore

Turning back to shore

⑧

⑦

⑥

Sheet out until the wave picks you up, then sheet in and head diagonally across the face of the wave. As the board picks up speed, lean forwards to keep your balance.

This is similar to conventional surfing. Position yourself about 5 - 10m ahead of the wave you intend to sail (avoid breaking waves to begin with).

The easiest way to turn back to shore is by gybing. The picture above shows a slam gybe. It is actually easier to gybe in waves because the swell of the wind helps you to turn in your desired direction.

*For safety's sake, do not sail further than about 300m from the shore.

37

Advanced waveriding and jumping

Advanced waveriding and jumping techniques are perhaps the most spectacular aspects of windsurfing. To attempt them, you will need to invest in a board designed specifically for wavesailing (see page 47). You also need supreme confidence in your basic wavesailing ability, as well as considerable nerve.

Conditions

The best conditions for these techniques are cross-shore winds of at least Force 4, steep waves which are at least one metre high and not much surf. Naturally, this combination provides a large element of risk, so observing both the routine safety tips on page 7, as well as the extra ones below, is vital.

Remember that most of the techniques shown here require many failed attempts before they are executed successfully.

Safety advice

1. Make sure that your footstraps are fitted correctly (see page 23), otherwise you may have difficulty getting free of your board if the jump goes wrong.

2. Always unhook your harness before attempting a jump. You need to be able to get as far away as possible from the board and rig if the jump fails.

3. If you feel your board getting out of control at any stage, take the following action:

i) Get out of the footstraps.

ii) Push the boom way from you.

iii) Jump away from the board and, if you have time, curl up in a ball before you hit the water.

iv) Swim to the board as soon as possible.

Advanced waveriding

The three techniques outlined below enable you to ride up, down and across a wave, as it is carrying you shorewards.

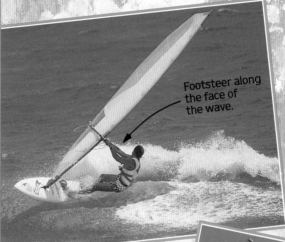

Footsteer along the face of the wave.

The cutback

This is a sharp turn made at the top of a wave. It then takes you back down the front of the wave to the point where it is starting to break. It is a good way to follow the rollercoaster.

Just before you reach the top of a wave, shift your weight to the back of the windward rail and sheet in. As you turn, transfer your weight towards the front of the board and quickly ride down the wave.

The rollercoaster

The rollercoaster involves turning into the wind as you reach the bottom of a wave, then sailing back up to the top again.

As the board accelerates down the front of the wave, move your weight back over the rear of the board to stall it. Then turn the nose of the board into the wind to climb back up to the top again.

Move your weight to the inner rail.

The bottom turn

This is made at the bottom of a wave in order to bear away crossways along its face.

Sail down the face of the wave on a broad reach. Bear away from the wind as if you were about to gybe, leaning into the turn and putting your weight on the inner rail.

Sheet out and keep the rig forward as you travel along the bottom of the wave.

Advanced jumps

To get airborne for an advanced jump, you use the same technique as for chop jumping (see page 37). From then on, the height, length and agility of the jump depend upon the steepness of the waves and your skill at manoeuvring the board.

Long jump

Take off as for chop jumping. When the nose of the board is airborne, pull the rig back a little, sheet in and squat down so that the board levels off, rather than going any higher into the air. To land nose first*: pull your back leg up towards your bottom and direct your front foot downwards. As you re-enter the water, lean backwards to level the board. To land tail first: sheet out slightly, straighten your legs and shift your weight to the back of the board.

Squat low to keep board level.

Lift windward rail to gain height.

High jump

Take off as for chop jumping. As soon as you are in the air, use your front foot to lift the windward rail, allowing the wind to get under the board and lift it higher. Crouch down, hang on to the boom and use your back foot to pull the tail of the board up under your buttocks.

Now prepare to land tail first (see above). Height, rather than length is the priority for this jump, so this type of landing is as effective as (and easier to execute than) a nose-first one.

Upside-down jump

The idea of this jump is to kick the board high into the air so that it turns upside-down through 180°, descending through the same arc, to land tail first. Take off as for the chop jump, but on a large wave which is about to break. As you take off, lean as far back as you can and pull up your front foot sharply. As the tail lifts, kick the board over your head into the wind, with the nose pointing downwind.

Kick the board over your head, into the wind.

Hang on to the boom as the board turns upside-down. When the tip of the rig touches the water, shift your weight quickly to the back of the board. As the board comes down, straighten your back leg and bend your front one to land softly, tail first.

Problem box

Problem The board starts to slip sideways during waveriding, or at the start of a jump.
Solution This is known as spin-out**. It is caused by a large amount of air getting underneath the board, particularly around the skeg, making it very unstable. To cure it, push the mast track forwards and shift your weight further towards the front of the board.

*A nose-first landing will give your jump greater length, but it is easier to land tail first.
**Spin-out can also be a problem when sailing at very high speeds on flat water. The solution is the same.

Windsurfing competitively

Rules about your equipment

The size and shape of a board and sail can make an enormous difference to the results of a competition. For this reason, most events specify a particular board and sail which can be used,*or specify the maximum measurements permitted.

Make sure you check this out before entering any windsurfing event or you could be disqualified before the starting gun has even gone off.

Course racing

Course races normally involve sailing around a triangular or 'W' course, shown below. An event may involve three or more races around the same course, and for each race competitors score points according to their placings. The eventual winner is the person who scores the lowest number of points overall.

1. Triangular course

This course is also known as the Olympic triangle as it was first used for dinghy races in the Olympics. The starting line always faces into the wind.

2. 'W' course

This differs from the triangular course in that there is no run, less upwind work, more gybes and more reaches. For this reason, the boards used tend to have less volume which makes them very efficient when reaching and gybing.

Slalom racing

This is normally held from a beach in very strong wind. The course consists of between two and six buoys laid in breaking surf, with the starting and finishing points on the beach. There is normally a series of heats leading to a final between four or five competitors.

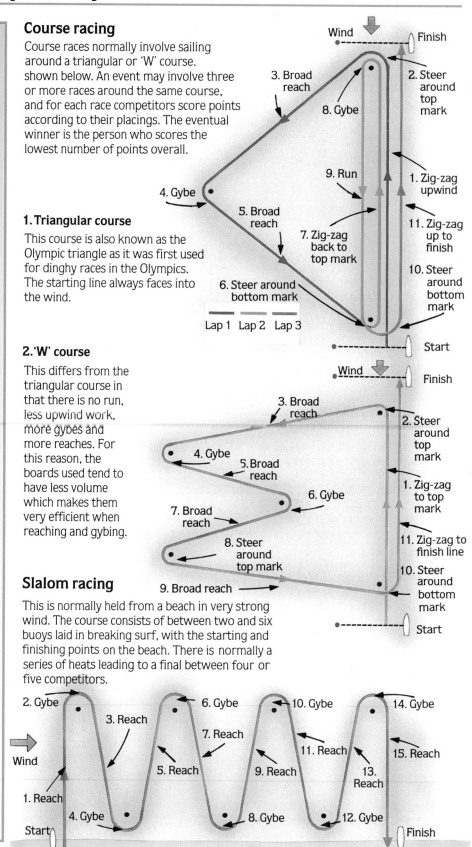

*This is known as a one-design event.

Wavesailing

Most wavesailing competitions involve a number of heats, each lasting for approximately seven minutes.

In each heat, four or five competitors try to impress the judges with their own series of wave jumping, riding and turning manoeuvres.

▲ Competitors make up their own jumping sequence.

Freestyle

Like wavesailing, competitors have a set amount of time to perform a routine in front of a panel of judges. One of the most popular types of competition is knockout freestyle. Everyone starts together in front of the judges who shout out tricks for them to perform. Anyone who fails is disqualified and has to return to shore. The person remaining at the end is the winner.

In a speed sailing competition, participants race against the clock. ▼

▲ Competitors in a knockout freestyle event obey the judges' instructions.

Speedsailing

Speedsailing competitions involve racing against the clock rather than other competitors along a straight 500m course. For maximum speeds, the water must be very flat, and the wind must be offshore* and very strong.

The fastest time on record is 38.86 knots (almost 71 kph) achieved in July 1986 by Pascal Maka in the Canary Islands. This beats the fastest time achieved by a dinghy which is 36 knots.

The world circuit

Below is a list of the most prestigious windsurfing events. They are organized by six major international windsurfing associations, as shown. To find out more about a particular event, write to the relevant association's address, given on page 60.

Annual events

Women's World Championships (IYRU)
Youth World Championships (IYRU)
Production Board World Championships (WBA)

Division II ** **European Championships** (IBSA)
Division II World Championships (IBSA)
Speedsailing events (WSSA)
Mistral European Championships (IMCO)
Mistral World Championships (IMCO)

Other events

Olympic Games (IYRU): each participating country can enter one windsurfing competitor.
World Tour (World Tour Events): began in 1988 with events throughout the world, including Europe, the USA, Australia and Japan.

Offshore winds reduce the amount of chop in the water.
**This is a racing division which has its own measurement rules.*

Entering a race

Entering your first windsurfing race can be very nerve-racking if you do not know the correct procedure and are not properly prepared for the event. These two pages take you through the build-up to a race, and also introduce you to some racing tactics.

Finding out about local races

One of the best ways to find out about suitable local races is to ask at your local windsurfing shop.

Alternatively, you could write to your national windsurfing authority (see page 60), who will be pleased to give you all the help they can. You need to find out the information on the right.

1. The name of the venue and the nearest large town to it.

2. The start time.

3. The types of boards being raced.

4. Whether buoyancy aids are compulsory.

The race numbers have been attached to the competitors' harnesses in this one-design event.

Sail numbers

For easy identification, you must have cloth sail numbers attached to the top third of both sides of your sail. Your national authority (see page 60) will issue you with a number which is yours for life. You can buy the sticky-back numbers from your local windsurfing shop. Stick them on to the sail when it is clean and dry. The numbers on the starboard side of the sail should be higher than those on the port side. At some one-design races*, the board and sail are provided for you. If so, stick your number on to your buoyancy aid or harness (see left).

Preparing your equipment

Make sure that everything is in good working order. In particular, check the universal joint and harness lines are not worn and about to break.

If you have a small sail, take it with you just in case of very strong winds. You will also need an accurate waterproof watch with a stop-watch

or countdown facility (see page 51) so that you can pace yourself in the final minutes before the start gun is fired.

At the race

Here is a guide to how you could spend the time before the race itself, from when you first arrive at the venue to the firing of the start gun.

 Arrive at the venue at least two hours before the starting time. Park close to the water so that you do not have far to carry your gear, and rig up immediately.

 Go to the club house and report to the race control (organizers). Give them your name, sail number, and insurance details.** You will also have to pay a small entry fee.

After the race: Analyse your performance and that of other competitors, and try to work out a way to do better next time. This is a good time to pick up tips by talking to your fellow competitors.

 When there are about ten seconds to go before the starting gun, start sailing as fast as you can. The aim is to cross the line at maximum speed immediately the start gun is fired.

 The five minute gun will go off to warn you that the race is about to start. This will be followed by the one minute gun. Check that your watch agrees with the gun; if not, reset it.

42   *See page 40.
**See page 61 for advice on choosing an insurance policy.

Racing tactics

Good windsurfing technique will not win you a race on its own. The top windsurfers are also brilliant tacticians. Here are a few basic tactics which could make a big difference to your results.

1 Which end of the start line?

On a triangular course, the start line is roughly at right angles to the upwind mark but rarely exactly so. This means that one end of the line is closer to the first mark than the other.

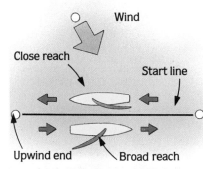

To find out which end is closest, sail from one end of the start line to the other, then back again. You will probably find that you had to sheet in further towards one end than the other. This will be the upwind, or favoured end.

However, you may find that a lot of people have chosen to start at the favoured end. If so, it is better to move down the line to find a space with cleaner wind (see right).

2 Windshifts

Because the wind direction is rarely constant, a good tactician will look out for windshifts and change course accordingly. This is particularly important on the upwind leg.

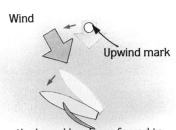

Here, the board has been forced to point lower. If the windsurfer tacks, it can point higher and sail more directly to the upwind mark.

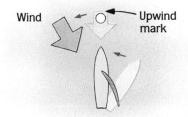

Here, the windshift has enabled the board to point higher. There is no need to tack.

How to spot a windshift

An experienced sailor can feel the wind shifting automatically. Alternatively, find a mark (such as a stationary boat) directly in line with your course. This is called a transit. If you suddenly find that you are sailing to one side of your transit, the wind has shifted.

3 Dirty wind

Dirty wind is windflow which has been disturbed by obstacles, in particular other people's sails. If you are sailing in dirty wind, your speed could be reduced by as much as 50%. It is therefore vital that you get a very good start and do not get stuck in another sailor's dirty wind. If you do become stuck, change tack to find a cleaner route.

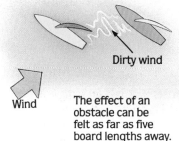

The effect of an obstacle can be felt as far as five board lengths away.

The race control will now brief you on the course and any potential hazards such as strong tides. If the course is complicated, draw it on the back of your hand.

The rescue team often wish to know the exact number of people on the water. Make sure you sign the safety list, and sign it again when you come ashore after the race.

Collect your equipment and sail out to the race area, checking your rig as you do so. In particular, make sure the boom is tight and at the right height.

The ten minute gun will now go off. Set the countdown on your watch. Sail to your chosen spot on the start line, and position yourself just behind it, on the starboard tack*.

Look at the course, familiarizing yourself with the positioning of each of the marks. Get the feel of the wind by sailing towards the upwind mark, then back again to the start line.

Now sail out to the start line. Use the method explained above to work out roughly where you wish to start on it. Then pick a stationary marker to help you remember it.

---

*See page 59 to work out which this is.

The speed sail and wind weapon

Windsurfing is an extremely fast-growing sport: improvements are being made to the equipment all the time to enable experts to go faster and do more spectacular manoeuvres. On top of this, some designers have been making more radical adjustments with the aim of combining windsurfing with other sports, such as skateboarding, skiing and even flying.

Two of the most exciting developments are the speed sail and wind weapon, both of which are shown here.

The speed sail

In the mid-1970s, French windsurfers Baron Arnaud de Rosnay and Herve Spriet decided to find a way of bringing the thrill and exhilaration of their sport to dry land. They came up with the speed sail in 1977, and in 1979 de Rosnay gave it a thorough test run by sailing it right across the Sahara Desert. Today there are more than 12,000 speed sailors around the world.

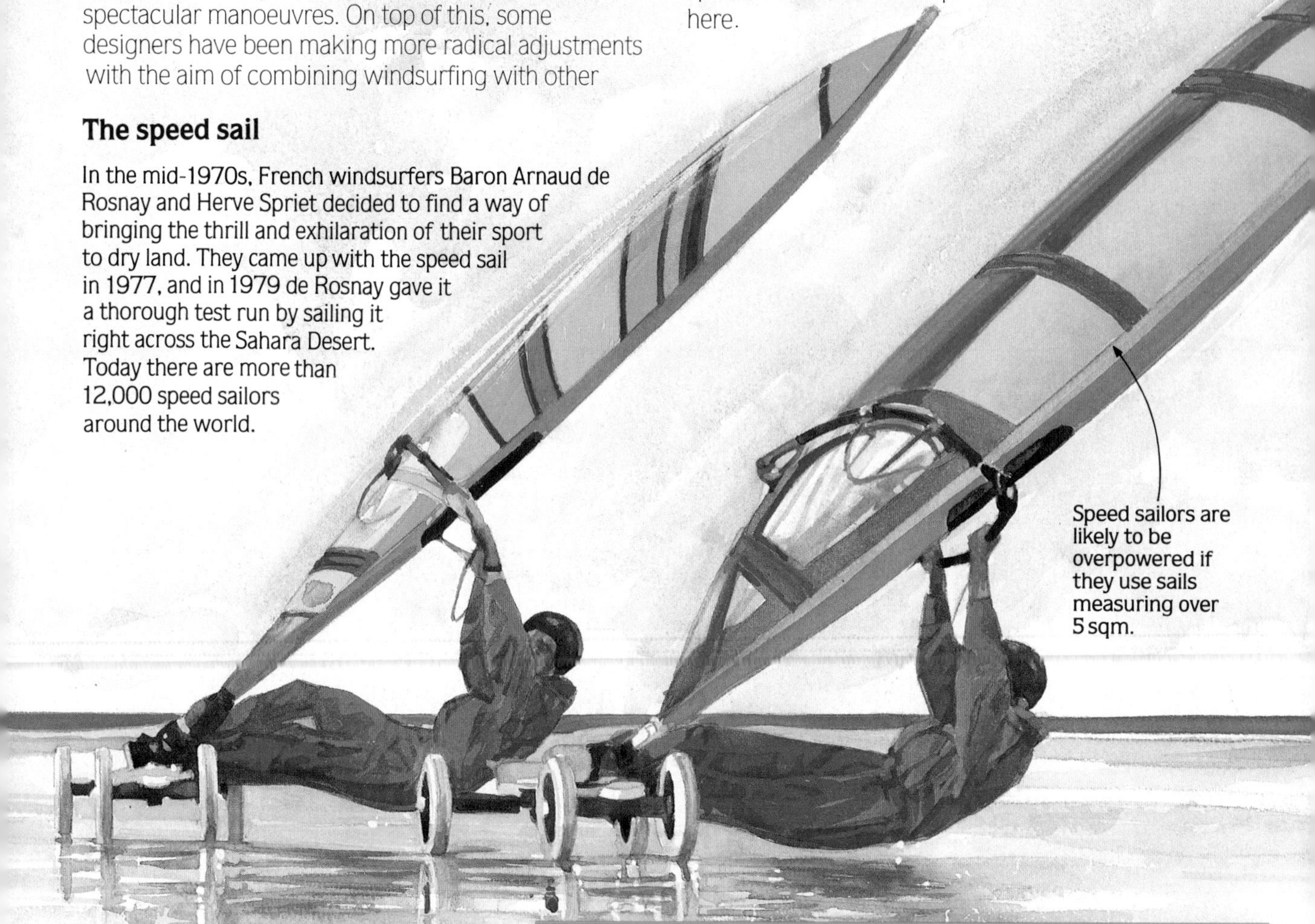

Speed sailors are likely to be overpowered if they use sails measuring over 5 sqm.

The speed sail consists of a normal windsurfing rig (not more than 5sqm) attached to a large version of a skateboard. The four wheels are on two axles which are padded for safety.*

You steer the speed sail using your body weight. The only problem is stopping: you either turn straight into the wind, or bale out. For this reason, most speed sailors protect themselves by wearing well-padded clothing and helmets, and by sailing on a sandy beach, rather than a harder surface. Winds required are less than those for normal windsurfing; most freestyle manoeuvres can be achieved in a Force 2 wind.

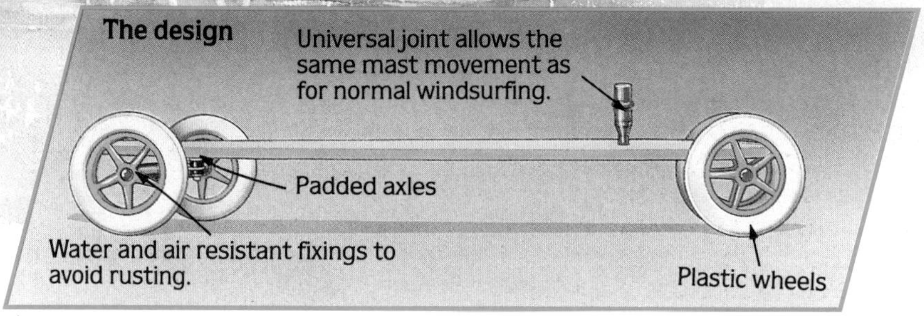

The design

Universal joint allows the same mast movement as for normal windsurfing.

Padded axles

Water and air resistant fixings to avoid rusting.

Plastic wheels

Speed sailing competitions

In 1983 the First Annual Speed Sailing World Championship was held in the Chott-el-Djerid, a dried-up lake in the heart of Tunisia, North Africa. Since then, venues have included Great Britain, the USA and Holland. Currently, about 100 speed sailors compete for the title of world champion every year.

The unofficial speed sailing record was set by Bruno Gouvy in August 1985: he reached 86.37mph (138.96kph) in Port St Louis, France. The official record of 45.84mph (73.75kph) is held by Jacques Sotty (June 1986, in Denneville, France).

*The original version is manufactured by Norbert Blanc sports (see page 60 for the address).

The wind weapon

The wind weapon can jump over 15m in height, and over 30m in length.

In 1983, Thomas Magruder (a veteran windsurfer) and Robert Crowell (a competition hang glider pilot) got together to discuss their common desire to combine their two sports. The end result was a type of windsurfer with a mast which is detached from the board. The sailor can pivot this, thereby transforming the sail into a horizontal wing.

It is possible to combine the top part of a wind weapon with the bottom part of a speed sail. If you get into trouble during a jump, the sail can be used as a kind of parachute to soften the board's landing.

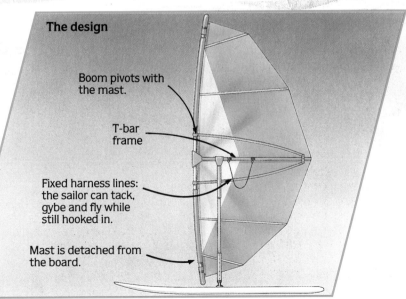

The design

Boom pivots with the mast.

T-bar frame

Fixed harness lines: the sailor can tack, gybe and fly while still hooked in.

Mast is detached from the board.

Choosing a board

It is easy to become confused by the jargon and marketing claims made by many windsurfing manufacturers. The information given on the following pages attempts to break through the jargon, enabling you to choose the right kind of equipment for your capabilities and ambitions.

The boards below have been grouped according to their length, as this affects the way they perform. However, it is important to remember that the weight of the sailor will also alter the way a board behaves on the water, and you must ensure that the board you choose has enough volume for you (see below).

Learner/light wind board (390-360cm)

This board is designed for beginners, providing stability and high volume to keep them afloat. Can pick up speed even in light winds.

Intermediate board for all conditions (380-360cm)

The design of this board makes it ideal for a more advanced sailor who wants to improve in light to medium wind speeds, or to race. Ambitious beginners might choose this board.

Intermediate/medium wind board (340-320cm)

A smaller version of the all-round long board, this board will need a stronger wind before it will start planing, but once moving will be faster and more manoeuvrable. Also, an ideal starter board for light adults.

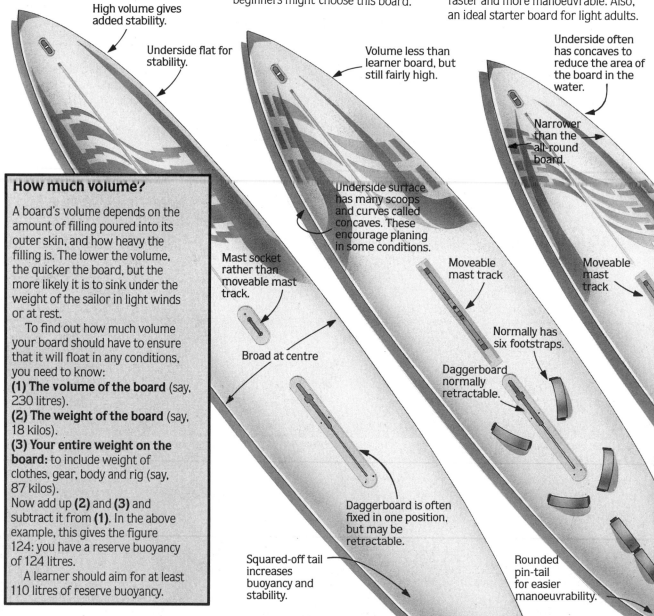

High volume gives added stability.

Underside flat for stability.

Volume less than learner board, but still fairly high.

Underside often has concaves to reduce the area of the board in the water.

Narrower than the all-round board.

Underside surface has many scoops and curves called concaves. These encourage planing in some conditions.

Mast socket rather than moveable mast track.

Broad at centre

Moveable mast track

Moveable mast track

Normally has six footstraps.

Daggerboard normally retractable.

Daggerboard is often fixed in one position, but may be retractable.

Squared-off tail increases buoyancy and stability.

Rounded pin-tail for easier manoeuvrability.

How much volume?

A board's volume depends on the amount of filling poured into its outer skin, and how heavy the filling is. The lower the volume, the quicker the board, but the more likely it is to sink under the weight of the sailor in light winds or at rest.

To find out how much volume your board should have to ensure that it will float in any conditions, you need to know:

(1) The volume of the board (say, 230 litres).
(2) The weight of the board (say, 18 kilos).
(3) Your entire weight on the board: to include weight of clothes, gear, body and rig (say, 87 kilos).

Now add up **(2)** and **(3)** and subtract it from **(1)**. In the above example, this gives the figure 124: you have a reserve buoyancy of 124 litres.

A learner should aim for at least 110 litres of reserve buoyancy.

Materials

Windsurfing boards are based on two components, the outer core (also known as the skin) and the filling inside the core. Board skins can be made out of glassfibre, polyethylene, ABS/ASA, or epoxy. The filling is normally polystyrene or polyurethane. These have varying qualities as shown below.

Skin	Stiffness	Impact strength	Weight	Long-term durability	Custom boards or mass-produced	Expense	Level of ability
Glassfibre (woven glass varnished with polyester or epoxy)	High	Medium	Very light	Low	Custom	Low	Advanced
Polyethylene (a type of plastic)	Low	High	Very heavy	High	Mass-produced	Low	All levels
ABS/ASA (different blends of plastic)	Medium	Medium	Medium	Medium	Mass-produced	Medium	All levels
Epoxy (resin blended with plastics or carbon fibre).	High	Low	Very light	Low	Both	High	Advanced
Filling							
Polyurethane (plastic foam, sometimes written PU)	——	Medium	Medium	High	Mass-produced	High	All levels
Polystyrene (expanded polystyrene plastic foam, sometimes written EPS)	——	Low	Light	Medium	Custom	Low	All levels

Intermediate high wind board (320-300cm)

The low volume of this board makes it ideal for speedsailing in strong winds. It is also an ideal beginner's board for a child.

Advanced high wind boards (295cm and below)

There are two types of design for boards of 295cm and below, depending on whether they are for wave sailing or speedsailing. Both are usually made to the specific demands of expert sailors*, although mass-produced versions are available. Their small volume means they sink easily at low speeds, hence the name "sinker".

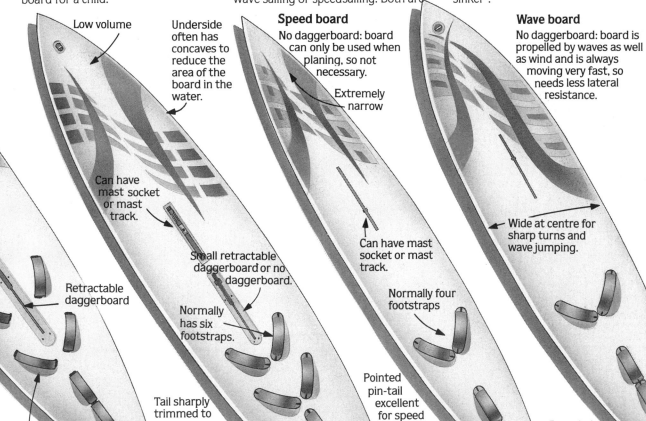

Low volume

Underside often has concaves to reduce the area of the board in the water.

Can have mast socket or mast track.

Retractable daggerboard

Six footstraps

Small retractable daggerboard or no daggerboard.

Normally has six footstraps.

Tail sharply trimmed to encourage speed and agility.

Speed board
No daggerboard: board can only be used when planing, so not necessary.

Extremely narrow

Can have mast socket or mast track.

Normally four footstraps

Pointed pin-tail excellent for speed but inhibits sharp turns.

Wave board
No daggerboard: board is propelled by waves as well as wind and is always moving very fast, so needs less lateral resistance.

Wide at centre for sharp turns and wave jumping.

Rounded pin-tail for tight turns.

*This is known as being custom-made.

Buying a rig

When buying a new board, you may be given a choice of rigs to go with it. Below is advice on choosing the right one for your level and strength. Each of the sails is available in a number of different sizes: basically, the lighter the wind, the larger the sail needed, although beginners should buy smaller sails which are easier to control and pull out of the water.

Once you are proficient you may wish to have more than one sail to suit the different wind conditions. If you do this, get advice from experts to ensure that the sail you choose will fit your boom and mast.

Recreational sail

This is known as a semi-soft sail because it has short battens, keeping the leech rigid enough for sailing in winds up to about Force 3, but leaving the middle of the sail free. This allows you to feel the wind in the sail, giving you good control in light winds, and the sail is light because it does not have the batten weight of a fully battened sail. It is therefore ideal for beginners, although also good for experts who wish to sail in light winds.

Semi-soft middle section

Rigid leech

Two short battens

Short, light-weight boom for easier handling.

Foot trimmed back to keep it clear of the water.

Fully battened sail

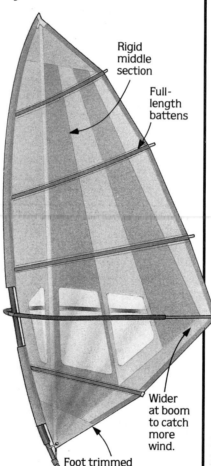

Rigid middle section

Full-length battens

Wider at boom to catch more wind.

Foot trimmed quite high.

This sail has battens which fit all the way across the sail and touch the mast. This produces a rigid sail which holds a better aerofoil shape* in gusty winds than the recreational sail. It is heavier than a recreational sail, though still manageable for the ambitious beginner, and more powerful.

Rotational asymmetrical foil (RAF) sail

Wide mast sleeve

Tapered battens allow sail to hold more wind at front of sail.

Sail wider at boom for extra power.

Foot trimmed high.

Here, the full-length battens can rotate around the back of the mast each time you change tack, allowing the sail to form an aerofoil shape* for that particular tack. This enables the wind to travel more smoothly along the leeward side of the sail than a normal fully battened sail allows.

The RAF sail is difficult for beginners to handle because of the large amount of power in the sail, and it is also heavy because the wide mast sleeve fills up with water when dropped.

*See page 11 for more about aerofoil shapes.

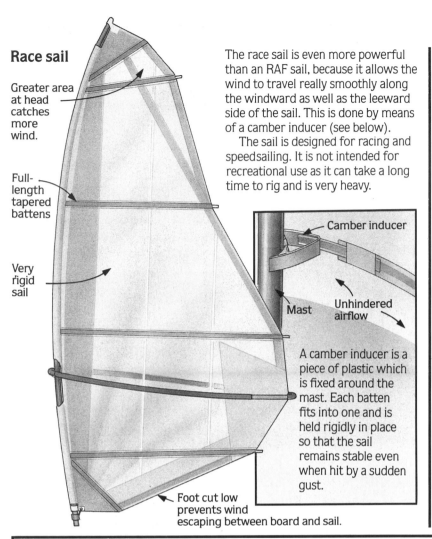

Race sail

Greater area at head catches more wind.

Full-length tapered battens

Very rigid sail

The race sail is even more powerful than an RAF sail, because it allows the wind to travel really smoothly along the windward as well as the leeward side of the sail. This is done by means of a camber inducer (see below).

The sail is designed for racing and speedsailing. It is not intended for recreational use as it can take a long time to rig and is very heavy.

Camber inducer

Mast

Unhindered airflow

A camber inducer is a piece of plastic which is fixed around the mast. Each batten fits into one and is held rigidly in place so that the sail remains stable even when hit by a sudden gust.

Foot cut low prevents wind escaping between board and sail.

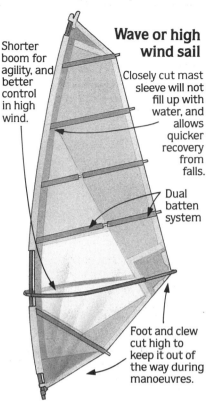

Wave or high wind sail

Shorter boom for agility, and better control in high wind.

Closely cut mast sleeve will not fill up with water, and allows quicker recovery from falls.

Dual batten system

Foot and clew cut high to keep it out of the way during manoeuvres.

Looks similar to an RAF sail, but has certain characteristics which provide better high wind control and allow greater agility. It has a dual batten system which allows you to use either long battens for added power or short battens for easier control.

Sail materials

Sail material has a great effect on how the sail performs. Below you can see three major materials in use today.

	Advantages	Disadvantages
Polyester Polyester is made by spinning strands of plastic with yarn and weaving cloth from the blended fibres. It is then heat-treated to produce a finish.	★ Cheap ★ Stretches to accommodate different mast curves. ★ Durable and easy to look after.	★ Absorbs water so relatively heavy. ★ Inefficient in high winds because it lacks rigidity.
Mylar Trade name for a number of clear, shiny materials made from a very thin polyester, such as Terylene, which is bonded to cloth. When bonded to both sides, it is brittle and very rigid. Some manufacturers just use it on the foot and leech where the stress is greatest.	★ Stays rigid in high winds and gusty conditions, so good for speed. ★ Light as it doesn't absorb water.	★ Expensive ★ Tears easily, and finish prone to damage. ★ Will only fit properly on one type of mast.
Polyester scrim A new development among manufacturers is to bond double-sided Mylar to polyester scrim (net) rather than cloth.	★ Very strong, so does not tear easily. ★ Very light. ★ Even more stable than traditional Mylar sail.	★ Expensive ★ Will only fit properly on one type of mast. ★ Requires greater looking after.

Windsurfing accessories

In addition to a board and rig, there are a number of accessories on the market. Some, such as the waterproof personal hi-fi, are optional extras, while others, such as the wetsuit or drysuit, are essentials.

Beware of falling into the image trap: you can have just as much fun on the water without spending a fortune on expensive shades and fashionable outfits, and you'll look much less silly when you fall off.

Buoyancy aids

These are designed to keep your upper body above the surface of the water. Make sure you choose one which has more buoyancy in the front than in the back so you are floated face up (this is called positive buoyancy). The amount of buoyancy an aid has is measured in kilos: look for one with at least six kilos.

Harnesses worn at the waist, chest or bottom have a small amount of buoyancy built into them. However, they will only float you on your front (negative buoyancy), or support the lower region of your body in the water.

Knapsacks and bumbags

These are available to wear on your back or bottom. Keep in it:

★ **A day-glo flag.** Waving one backwards and forwards over your head is a recognized distress signal.

★ **Two flares.** These can be seen from a great distance, even in bad visibility. Check the expiry dates.

★ **A whistle.** Sound travels very quickly over water.

★ **Some rope.** A piece of rope four metres long can be used for towing someone else, or being towed yourself. Also handy for emergency repairs.

★ **A knife.** This could save lives if you or someone else were caught in the rig and had to be cut free. Also useful for emergency repairs.

Wetsuits and drysuits

The major difference between a wetsuit and drysuit is that drysuits keep you warm by keeping you dry, whereas wetsuits trap water between your body and the suit. This heats up to your body temperature and creates a wet layer of insulation.

Drysuits

Drysuits can be worn with clothing underneath, so are ideal for winter windsurfing. They are the most expensive suit available and must be vented before use (see below).

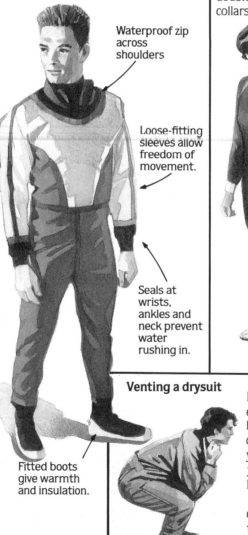

Waterproof zip across shoulders

Loose-fitting sleeves allow freedom of movement.

Seals at wrists, ankles and neck prevent water rushing in.

Fitted boots give warmth and insulation.

Wetsuits

These are close-fitting and usually worn over swimwear. The sleeves and legs are often thinner than the body of the suit to allow you flexible movement and prevent cramping. On most suits, knee and shin pads are added for durability.

There are several types of wetsuit. The dry steamer, steamer and long john are shown here.

Dry steamer

This type of wetsuit keeps you 80% dry which is sufficient for winter wear. You can buy them single- or double-lined (see right) with high collars or hoods.

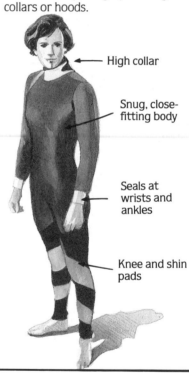

High collar

Snug, close-fitting body

Seals at wrists and ankles

Knee and shin pads

Venting a drysuit

It is essential to eliminate any excess air from inside your suit before you go sailing. This is called venting. If you do not, you will find it difficult to right yourself if you fall in: people have drowned in this way.

Pull open the neck seal, then crouch down. This will cause the air to rush out.

Steamer

Steamers allow in a lot more water than the dry steamer. This makes them cooler, so they are better suited to summer wear.

You can buy steamers which have removable arms and legs which allow you to cool off when the sun comes out. They are available both single- and double-lined (see below).

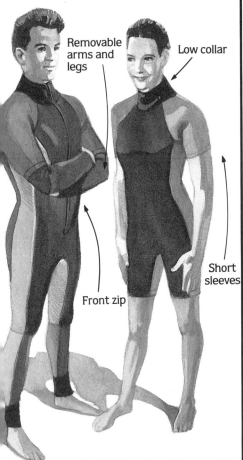

Removable arms and legs

Low collar

Front zip

Short sleeves

Single or double lining?

All wetsuits are made of neoprene. This can be layered on both sides with nylon (double-lined), to make them tougher. However, the nylon does tend to trap water more easily than neoprene, making the suit less efficient. Some suits, called smoothskins, are only lined on the inside and are therefore warmer though less durable.

Long john and jacket

This outfit is versatile because it can be worn with or without a jacket. However, water does get in between the jacket and the body so it is not suitable for winter use.

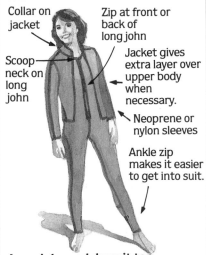

Collar on jacket

Scoop neck on long john

Zip at front or back of long john

Jacket gives extra layer over upper body when necessary.

Neoprene or nylon sleeves

Ankle zip makes it easier to get into suit.

Long john and drysuit top

This is the latest combination which can be used in most conditions. It consists of a smoothskin watertight long john with high waterproof neck and velcro straps around the ankles to stop water pushing up into the suit.

The drysuit top fits over the top of the long john in the colder winter months, and has seals at the neck and wrists. It is made from waterproof fabric.

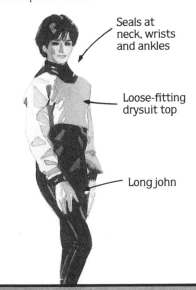

Seals at neck, wrists and ankles

Loose-fitting drysuit top

Long john

Winter extras

On cold days, you will need the following:

1. A hat. Neoprene hats are available, and you can buy suits with hoods attached, but any hat which is snug and secure is better than nothing.

2. Boots. Unless your suit has boots attached, it is advisable to buy long waterproof boots which fit snugly under the legs of your suit.

An alternative is dip-coated socks (socks dipped in neoprene or latex): these have thin soles which give the feel of bare feet, but keep you a lot warmer.

3. Gloves. Drysuit gloves or neoprene mittens will provide maximum warmth and protection, although rubber household gloves are a cheap alternative.

Summer extras

On hot days, you will need the following:

1. Sun tan lotion. The glare of the sun off the water can give you a severe sunburn. Exposed skin should be covered with waterproof, high protection sunscreen.

2. Glasses or visors. You must protect your eyes on bright glary days. Any polarized sunglasses which fit securely will do. You can buy an attachment that fits around your head to prevent them from falling off. Alternatively, a visor will keep the sun off the top of your face.

Other extras

Waterproof personal hi-fi. Make sure this has a strap attaching it to your neck.

Waterproof watch. For racing, look for one with a countdown feature, a clear read-out and a safety strap. It should be easy to use in the winter when you may be wearing bulky gloves, and should also be knock-resistant.

Make sure the watch you choose is waterproof rather than water resistant: the latter is only designed to survive splashes.

Caring for your equipment

By looking after your windsurfing equipment, you can ensure that it gives you years of pleasure, and increase its second-hand value should you wish to trade it in.

Below are a few tips on how to prolong the life of your gear. There is also advice on what to look out for if you are buying second-hand equipment.

The board

Rinse it out to get rid of salt sticking to the surface, and ensure that the daggerboard slot and mast track are free from sand and grit.

If you get stubborn stains on the board, for example, tar, scrub at it using a household cleaner. As a last resort, dab a little white spirit or petrol on a piece of cloth, and rub the stain with it using small, circular movements.

Check the skeg and daggerboard regularly for signs of wear. It is a good idea to sand the edges down regularly to keep them smooth; this is particularly important before you go freestyling.

The rig

Rinse the rig thoroughly after sailing in the sea, otherwise salt will stick to the sail and the stitching will rot. Loosen the tension on the battens, downhaul and outhaul, then leave the sail to dry on the mast.
Make sure it is thoroughly dry before removing the sail from the mast and rolling it up, starting from the top.

Remove all the sand and grit from the mast foot and the inside of the mast by rinsing it thoroughly. Failure to do this will result in a mast foot and mast which are firmly stuck together.

Finally, if you have them, make sure you clean mast and boom extensions thoroughly.

Wetsuits and drysuits

Salt can damage neoprene very easily, so always rinse wetsuits and drysuits thoroughly and dry them on a hanger, inside out (this will lessen the risk of your having to put on a damp suit). Put powder on drysuit seals to keep them supple and easy to use next time around.

Equipment checklist

Before going out on the water, make the following checks:

★ Are there any nicks or holes in the board? If so, do not sail the board until you have made at least a temporary repair. If the foam inside the board gets wet, the board will become very heavy and difficult to repair. As a short-term measure, cover the hole with water-resistant tape.

Solution For a lasting repair, either buy a repair kit and follow the manufacturer's instructions, or get a professional to do the repair for you.

★ Are there any rips in the sail? Small nicks can become gaping tears if they are not repaired immediately.

Solution Either sew it up yourself using nylon yarn, or get it done professionally.

★ Are any of the ropes looking worn?

Solution Replace them with new ones, burning the ends with a flame first to prevent them from fraying.

★ Check the universal joint for signs of stress. This is subjected to an enormous amount of pressure, and may easily snap while you are out on the water.

Solution If in doubt, replace it with a new one.

★ Check your wetsuit or drysuit for tears.

Solution You can mend small nicks using patches and glue from a special repair kit (alternatively, a cycle repair kit is useful if you are stuck), but larger tears should be treated by a professional.

Storage solutions

Windsurfing equipment is very large, particularly the mast and board, and can cause enormous storage problems. How you solve the problems will depend on the space available, but here are a few tips:

★ Storage racks are a useful way of keeping your equipment out of the way, ideally in a garage.

★ If possible, lay the board horizontally. This saves it from having to take too much weight on one end. Likewise, stack sails horizontally; stacking them vertically may cause the material to crack.

★ A large variety of specialist bags are available for storing different items of equipment, such as your board and daggerboard (see right) . These are particularly useful for transporting your equipment, as well as for storing it outside. Make sure you choose a board bag which is well-padded: it will then protect the board from the elements and from small knocks.

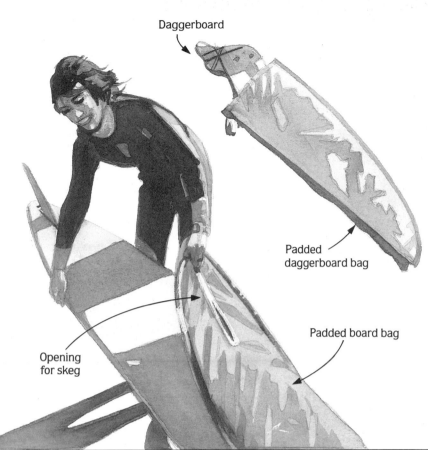

Daggerboard

Padded daggerboard bag

Padded board bag

Opening for skeg

Buying second-hand

Buying your equipment second-hand can be an excellent way to save money, but there are some risks involved. It is essential that you can tell whether the equipment is in good condition, or whether it is wearing out. Below are a few tell-tale signs to look out for.

★ Soft spots in the board. This indicates that the foam filling has begun to come away from the outer skin. This can cause splits in the seam and delamination, which is a major problem.

★ Damage and cracks in the boom end, universal joint, and any large cracks in the mast. Small cracks in the mast can be repaired, but elsewhere cracks will mean putting in a new part.

★ Worn out or damaged mast foot wells or castings: these could prevent you from removing the mast foot from the mast, and will need replacing.

★ Kinks in the mast or boom, or a seriously torn boom grip. The boom grip can be replaced, but the kinks are a major problem.

★ Any sail which is so baggy that it cannot be properly tensioned: this cannot be repaired, and will severely affect your performance.

The second-hand market

Notice-boards and classified advertisements in windsurfing magazines are cheap sources of second-hand equipment. However, there are more risks involved: you are unlikely to be given a guarantee, or a refund later if something goes wrong.

Dealers, on the other hand, are legally obliged to provide you with a guarantee with second-hand equipment, although they will normally charge a higher price than a private seller.

Whoever you buy from, do not agree a deal without taking the equipment out for a test sail: this should include rigging the equipment yourself (see pages 54-55).

Rigging

It is very important to rig your windsurfer correctly so that it does not come apart when you are sailing. These two pages explain how to rig your windsurfer correctly to ensure good performance on the water.

If you are hiring your windsurfing equipment, check that it has been properly rigged using the checklist on the opposite page.

Unroll the sail and spread it on the ground. Push the mast into the sail sleeve, making sure that the top of the mast (the thinner end) goes into the top of the sail. Now take the mast foot and fit it into the bottom of the mast.

Thread the downhaul line through the bottom of the sail then back into the mast foot. Repeat, finishing off by going through the cleat of the mast foot. If you have a pulley, use it as shown above.* Tension the downhaul slightly.

Now work out the correct positioning for the boom. Stand the mast and sail up by your side and note the point which is around shoulder-height. Mark this with a piece of waterproof tape: this will make rigging quicker next time.

Derigging

Always derig in the following order:

1. Release tension on battens.

2. Release downhaul.

3. Release outhaul.

If you release the outhaul before the downhaul, you could severely damage the sail. Remember the saying: "down and out".

Stand the mast up and pull the boom down so that it is at right angles to the mast. If you have tied your inhaul correctly, the two should be secured tightly to ensure that it does not slip down when sailing. If it does not feel secure, retie the inhaul.

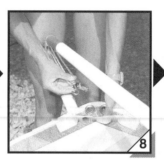

Now attach the clew (the far corner of the sail) to the outer end of the boom with the outhaul line, using a pulley if you have one.* Again, the way you should do this will depend on what design of boom end fitting you have.

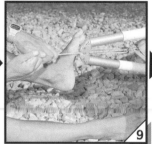

Tightly tension the outhaul. This can be difficult to do: a good tip is to sit on the ground and use your foot to help you. It is important to tension the outhaul well so that you will be able to tension the battens correctly later.

Adjusting the sail shape

The amount of tension you have in your sail should vary according to the wind strength. In light winds, you need a full shape to allow more wind in the sail. However, when it is stronger, you want to reduce the power of the wind, so the sail should be well-tensioned to give it a flatter shape.

Full sail shape for light wind conditions

Flat sail shape for strong wind conditions

Whatever the wind strength, ensure that the downhaul is tight enough to avoid any horizontal creases in the sail. This makes it easier to control, and bends the mast so that the sail sets easily on either side. Also, check that the outhaul is tight enough to stop the sail touching the boom.

*Using a pulley will make it easier to tension the downhaul and outhaul.

Because the boom has to be very tightly attached to the mast, it is possible to damage, or even crack the mast. To reduce the chances of doing this, you can buy a mast protector which slots on to the mast, underneath the boom.

Next, feed the boom around the top of the mast and sail until it is level with your mark, or over your mast protector. The top knot on the uphaul should face towards the top of the mast. Lie the boom parallel to the mast.

Use the inhaul to attach the boom to the mast. There are many different ways of doing this, depending on the design of your boom end. Follow your manufacturer's instructions, or ask your dealer if you are unsure.

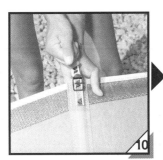

Push each batten right to the end of its slot using the palm of your hand. The outer end of the batten should be inside the strap on the sail. Use your other hand to pull the strap away from you, then sharply pull it towards you.

Now tension the sail to suit the conditions (see below). This normally involves tightening the downhaul (again, sit down and use a foot to help you do this) and slackening the outhaul. Tie off the outhaul and downhaul ropes.

Tie the free end of the shock cord to the bottom of the uphaul. Now attach the uphaul to the mast foot by looping the other end of the shock cord around the mast foot, and fastening it with the hook, as shown in the above photograph.

Attaching a tow loop

If you find yourself in trouble and need a tow back to shore, or wish to help another distressed windsurfer, you will have a much easier job if you have had the foresight to attach a tow loop to your towing eye. You can then attach a tow rope to this, rather than try to thread a rope which is too thick through a wet towing eye.

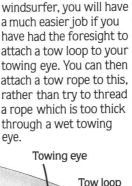

Towing eye

Tow loop

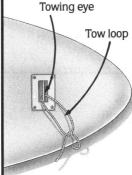

All you need is a thin piece of rope, approximately 20cm long. Thread it through the towing eye, then knot the two ends securely together.

Checklist when hiring equipment

Although there are some very good windsurfing schools and clubs which hire out very good equipment, there are also, unfortunately, a number of irresponsible outfits. On page 53 you can find out how to check whether equipment is in good condition; below are things you should check to ensure it is well-rigged.

★ Is the boom at the right height for you?

★ Is the boom securely fastened to the sail?

★ Are the outhaul and downhaul securely fastened?

★ Is the sail correctly tensioned for the conditions?

★ Are the battens securely tensioned?

★ Is it the right size for you and the conditions? In particular, if the wind is quite strong and you are unsure, go for a small, semi-soft sail rather than a fully battened one (see pages 48-49).

Some useful knots

Two knots that are useful to learn are the bowline and figure of eight, shown below.

Bowline: good for any occasion when you need a loop which can easily be undone.

Figure of eight: good as a locking knot at the end of the outhaul, downhaul and uphaul.

Transporting your windsurfer

Unless you live, or are staying, within easy walking distance of a beach or lake, you will probably have to transport your windsurfer to your chosen venue by car. Below you can find out how to adapt a normal roof-rack to carry a windsurfer safely.

When driving with a windsurfer on top, make sure you make allowances for the length of the mast so you don't hit anything.

Things you need

★ A car roof-rack.

★ A pair of quick-release straps.

★ A mast attachment which fits your roof-rack (you can buy this from a windsurfing shop).

★ A length of strong rope.

★ Some insulating tape or foam (you can buy specially shaped foam bars from windsurfing shops).

★ Some scraps of day-glo fabric.

Attaching the board and rig to the roof-rack

1. If the roof-rack has sharp edges which might damage your windsurfer, wrap foam or insulating tape around them. Alternatively, put the foam bars across the roof-rack, about one metre apart.

2. If you are on your own, rest the deck of your board against your car, with the tail on the ground. Now slide the board on to the rack until the nose protrudes forwards as much as the tail protrudes backwards. If you have a friend to help you, it is easier to lift the board straight on to the roof-rack.*

3. Place the boom on top of the board, with any protrusions on the boom facing upwards so they do not damage the board. Put the sail in its sailbag and position it inside the boom.

4. Fasten the mast attachments to each end of one side of the roof-rack (make sure that they are screwed on really tightly, so they do not slip when the car is moving). Position the mast inside them and fasten the rubber attachment around it.

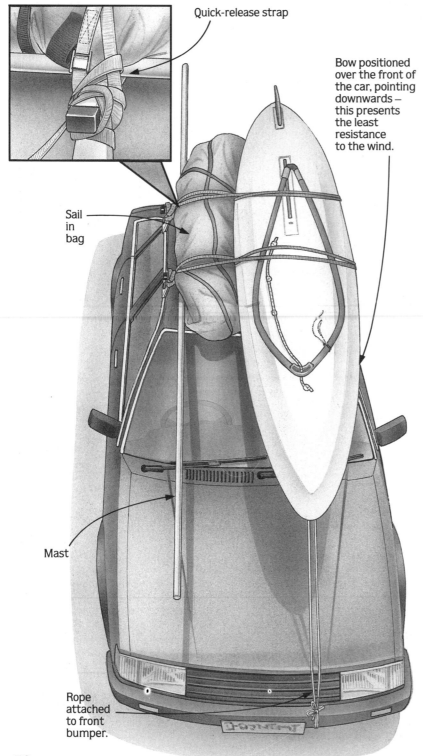

Quick-release strap

Bow positioned over the front of the car, pointing downwards – this presents the least resistance to the wind.

Sail in bag

Mast

Rope attached to front bumper.

56

*In fact, some long boards are too heavy for one person to carry alone, so help may be essential.

5. Take one of the quick-release straps and lash it under the roof-rack and over the top of the equipment, near the front of the rack.

6. Do the same with the other strap, towards the back end of the rack. Tighten both straps, then wrap the ends once round the mast, then around the roof-rack, and knot them securely.

7. Thread one end of your rope through the towing eye* on the front of the board and pull it half-way through. Pulling the rope really taut, tie the ends together around the front bumper of the car.

8. If the mast sticks out at either end of the car, bind a piece of day-glo fabric around the protruding bits so that they can be seen easily.

Locking up

It is a good idea to lock your equipment on to your roof-rack if it is going to be out of your sight for some time.

One of the most secure locking devices on the market is called the Board Guard. The cable is sold with attachments which fit into either the board or rig (see below).

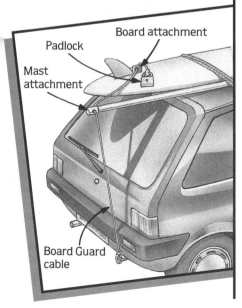

Board attachment

Padlock

Mast attachment

Board Guard cable

Carrying your windsurfer to the water

It is easier to carry your board and sail to the water's edge separately. Start with your board, but make sure that you do not leave your sail in a vulnerable place, as it could get blown away. Position your board by the water's edge, upside-down (to avoid damaging the skeg) and pointing into the wind, then go back for your sail.

Place your sail in the water first, as it is less likely to float very far away.

Carrying the board

Either:
Turn your board on its side with the deck towards you. Face the front of the board and pick it up by placing your left hand in the mast socket and your right hand in the daggerboard slot.

Or:
Put your daggerboard into the slot. Put your right hand over the board, and hold the daggerboard from the front. In this way, you can use it to help you carry the board (see above).

Carrying your rig

Here are two methods for carrying your rig, both of which involve using the rig to help you. If you find that the wind is impeding your progress, you are probably doing something wrong.

Either:

1. Lay the rig on the ground with the mast at 90° to the wind.

2. Stand behind the mast with your back to the wind.

3. Put one hand on the mast, just above the boom, and the other hand on the boom.

4. Lift the rig and walk to the water, keeping the mast at 90° to the wind.

Or:

1. Again, place the rig on the ground with the mast at right angles to the wind.

2. Now lift the sail up above your head, positioning the mast horizontally in front of you.

3. One hand should be supporting the mast and the other hand supporting the boom, underneath the sail.

*If you have put a loop of rope through the towing eye (see page 55), secure the rope to this.

Wind and tides

It is important to assess the wind before you go windsurfing so that you know whether you can cope with the conditions, and if so, what equipment you need to take. You can do this by looking at its effect on trees, water and so on, or by measuring it with an anemometer. Alternatively, you can listen to the shipping forecasts or telephone the local weather centre. One system used to indicate the strength of the wind is the so-called British Beaufort scale, shown below.

Force	State of wind	State of sea	State on land	Wind speed
0	Calm	Like a mirror	Smoke rises vertically.	Under 1 knot*
1	Light air	Ripples	Smoke drifts with wind.	1-3 knots
2	Light breeze	Small wavelets which may have crests.	Wind felt on face, leaves rustle.	4-6 knots
3	Gentle breeze	Large wavelets with breaking crests. May be scattered white horses.	Leaves and small twigs constantly moving. Wind extends light flags.	7-10 knots
4	Moderate breeze	Small waves to fairly frequent white horses.	Lifts dust and loose paper. Moves small branches.	11-16 knots
5	Fresh breeze	Moderate waves forming many white horses. Maybe some spray.	Small trees begin to sway. Crested wavelets on lakes and reservoirs.	17-21 knots
6	Strong breeze	Large waves with white foam crests. Probably some spray.	Large branches moving. Difficult to use umbrellas.	22-27 knots
7	Near gale	Sea heaps up. Some white foam from breaking waves blowing in direction of wind.	Whole trees in motion. Quite difficult to walk against wind.	28-33 knots**
8	Gale	Moderately high waves. Well-marked streaks of foam moving with wind.	Twigs breaking off trees.	34-40 knots
9	Severe gale	High waves. Dense streaks of foam and confused breaking crests. Spray may affect visibility.	Branches breaking off trees.	41-47 knots
10	Storm	Very high waves with long overhanging crests. Surface of water is white. Visibility affected.	Trees uprooted. Considerable structural damage.	48-55 knots
11	Violent storm	Extremely high waves hide ships.	Large buildings start to move.	56-63 knots
12	Hurricane	Air full of driving spray. Very bad visibility.	Large buildings may collapse.	Over 63 knots

*A knot is equivalent to approximately 1.15mph or 1.85kmph.
**Above 30 knots, even an expert windsurfer could not sail very effectively.

Wind direction

As well as indicating the strength of the wind, a weather forecast will tell you its direction. A southerly wind, for example, is a wind coming from the south. This is extremely useful as, by lining up a compass on a large-scale map, you will be able to tell in advance which venues are likely to have cross-shore or diagonally onshore winds. However, you should also take into account the effect of sea and land breezes (see right).

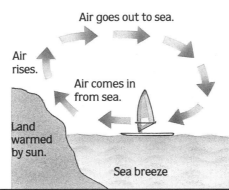

Air goes out to sea.

Air rises.

Air comes in from sea.

Land warmed by sun.

Sea breeze

On warm days, the land heats up more quickly than the sea. This causes the air to rise over the land and air moves in from the sea to replace it. This is known as a sea breeze and, in very hot weather, can have the effect of a Force 4 onshore wind.

On the other hand, the land cools down in the evening more quickly than the sea, causing an offshore wind which can be hazardous to the unprepared.

Tides

Tides are caused by the gravitational pull of the moon and sun. The strength of the tide depends upon the position of the sun in relation to the moon, as shown in the diagrams below.

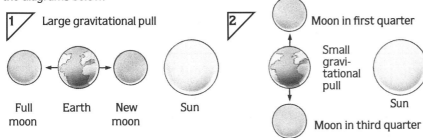

1 Large gravitational pull

Full moon — Earth — New moon — Sun

2 Moon in first quarter

Small gravitational pull

Sun

Moon in third quarter

Sun and moon in line: pull is greatest. This is known as a spring tide.

It takes about six hours for the tide to change from a high tide (when the water is in) to a low tide (when it is out). Of the six hour cycle, the effect of the tide is strongest during the

Sun and moon at right angles: pull is smallest. This is known as a neap tide.

middle two hours. Never windsurf in an outgoing spring tide, especially during its middle two hours. If the wind dropped, you would simply be swept out to sea.

Checking the state of the tide

In most coastal areas, local tide tables are available from newsagents, for example. These will tell you the times of all the tides for every day of the year.

If you are unable to obtain a tide table, follow the basic tips outlined below in order to work out whether the tide is coming in or going out.

1. Look at the beach. If it is dry, the tide is coming in. If it is wet, the tide is going out.

2. Unless there is a very strong wind, anchored boats will position themselves to face towards the direction of the tide.

Rules of the water

Just as there are strict driving laws for road-users to prevent accidents, there are also rules to avoid collisions on the water. The basic rules of the water are shown here. Obviously, the most important thing is to use your common sense: if you see a large ship or a novice windsurfer coming towards you, take steps to get out of the way.

1. A board on starboard tack has right of way over one on port tack. An easy way to tell which tack you are on is by identifying which shoulder is closest to the mast.

★ Board on starboard tack: right shoulder closest to the mast.
★ Board on port tack: left shoulder closest to the mast.

2. An overtaking board must keep clear.

3. When both boards are on the same tack, the board closest to the wind (on the windward side) must give way to a board which is on the leeward side.

Racing rules

In addition to the basic rules described on the left, there are many rules designed for racing. There is a whole rulebook specifically for racing, but the three most important rules are described below.

1. A board that is tacking or gybing must keep clear of one that is not turning.

2. Normally, at any of the marks, the board on the inside should be given room to round the mark.

3. A board has no rights if it sails backwards across the start line.

Wavesailing rules

There are a number of additional rules designed to prevent collisions on the waves.

1. A board riding towards the shore has right of way over one sailing out to sea.

2. When two boards are riding the same wave, the board nearest the break has right of way.

3. When two boards are riding different waves, the board furthest from shore has right of way.

4. Windsurfers give way to surfers when there is a danger of collision.

Going further

If you are thinking about going on a windsurfing holiday or joining a club, you will find the information below to be of use. There are also suggestions of specialist books to read and the addresses of some major windsurfing organizations.

Books

General

Windsurfing: Improving techniques
Ben Oakley
The Crowood Press
(Available only in the UK)

The complete guide to windsufing
(Revised edition)
Jeremy Evans
Unwin Hyman
(Published in the USA under the imprint Facts on File)

Racing

Start to win
Eric Twiname
Adlard Coles Ltd
Published in the USA under the imprint Sheridan House

Slalom (The sailboard book skill guide series)
Reed Lockhart
Grubb Media Ltd
(Available in the USA and UK under the same imprint)

Windsurfing race tactics
Noel Swanson
Stanford Maritime

Racing rules
World sailboard manufacturers' association

Freestyle

Freestyle windsurfing
Roger Jones and Gary Eversole
Pelham books

Understanding the weather

Weather lore for sailors and windsurfers
Gunther Roth
EP- A & C Black

Spotter's guide to the weather
F. Wilson and F. Mansfield
Usborne Publishing
(Distributed in the USA by EDC)

Dinghy and boardsailing weather
Alan Watts
A & C Black

Useful addresses

Below are the addresses of some major windsurfing organizations. They are invaluable sources of information about local venues, races, courses and so on.

UK

Royal Yachting Association
RYA House
Romsey Road
Eastleigh
Southampton
Hampshire

United Kingdom Boardsailing Association
Masons Road
Stratford-upon-Avon
Warwickshire

British Windsurfing Association
163 West Lane
Hayling Island
Hampshire

Canada

Canadian Yachting Association
333 River Road
Vanier, Ottawa
Ontario K1L 8B9

USA

United States Boardsailing Association
PO Box 206
Oyster Bay, NY 117711

San Fransisco Boardsailing Association
2174 Union Street Box 47
San Fransisco
CA 94123

San Diego Boardsailing Association
1930 First Avenue
San Diego
CA 92101

New Zealand

New Zealand Yachting Federation
PO Box 4173
Auckland

Australia

Australian Yachting Federation
33 Peel Street
Milson's Point
NSW 2061

International organisations

World Boardsailing Association, World Tour Events, International Funboard Association and Professional Boardsailing Association are all at:

Feldafinger Platz 2
71 Munchen 8000
Germany

World Speedsailing Association
PO BOX 351
Hove
Sussex, BN3 2PW
Great Britain

International Mistral Association
Grindel Strasse 11
8303 Bassendorf
Switzerland

Norbert Blanc Sports
15, av. Pierre 1er de Serbie
75116 Paris
France

Holidays

Although there are no guarantees for future wind and weather conditions, you can find out what is most likely for a particular venue at the time of year you plan to travel. Below are the normal weather patterns for some popular venues. For more detailed information contact your local weather centre for their latest international information.

The Mediterranean normally offers good conditions for the beginner to intermediate with warm water and good sea breezes in the summer. Some popular spots are Minorca, Sardinia, Turkey, Tunisia and the Greek islands. Tarifa in Spain is one of the best-known windsurfing venues for experts. However, it is not a place for beginners as winds average Force 6 for most of the year.

The Caribbean is ideal for both the intermediate and expert. The south coast of Barbados offers the best conditions with a cross shore wind and offshore reef break (good for wave jumping). The winter months (particularly the last two weeks of December and the first two weeks of January) are slightly more reliable for wind with a daily breeze of around Force 4-5, however this can also be expected three or four days a week in the summer months.

Hawaii offers very good windsurfing conditions for all standards of windsurfer. However, the wind conditions are not as reliable as Tarifa, Barbados or Perth.

Perth, Australia has perfect windsurfing conditions for the intermediate to experts during the months December to February. Sea breezes reach an average of Force 5-6 in the afternoon.

The Canary islands are probably the most popular of all European windsurfing holiday locations. From May to August you can expect north-easterly winds of Force 4-5. Lanzarote and Fuerteventura are the most popular islands.

The Great Lakes have good winds and choppy waves in the summer. Lake Simcoe is less rough and more suitable for beginners. Vancouver Island on the Atlantic coast is good for wave sailing.

Package deal holidays

Before making a booking, ask your travel agent the following questions:

★ How many students per instructor? Six is considered manageable.

★ What is the range of equipment?

★ Is the equipment in good condition, or old and worn out?

★ Are there enough boards for the number of holiday-makers? It is very frustrating to have to queue for a board.

Taking your own board

Many people prefer to take their own equipment with them on holiday. Here are a few tips.

1. Equipment can easily be damaged in transit. Protect your board by putting it in a quality board bag (these can be bought or hired). Alternatively, cover it with two layers of bubble pack, and tape the boom and sails to the deck. Also cover both ends of the mast. It helps if you can take a two-piece mast.

2. If travelling by air, check with the airline that there is enough room in the holds to carry your equipment. If possible, get confirmation of this in writing, and take the letter with you to the airport in case there are problems. You may have to pay an excess baggage fee; check this in advance to ensure there are no nasty surprises at the airport. Get to the airport early.

3. Check that your insurance is valid (see right).

Joining a club

Here are some of the advantages of joining a club:

★ You will meet like-minded enthusiasts and be able to exchange information and tips.

★ You can buy and sell second-hand equipment through the club noticeboard.

★ You will be able to take part in organized races with other club members of a similar standard.

★ Many clubs provide clubhouse facilities, including changing areas, showers and refreshments.

★ Some clubs offer storage space for your board and rig.

Insurance policies

It is a very good idea to insure your board and equipment as soon as you get it. As well as giving you peace of mind, it is often compulsory for racers. Below are the main things to look for in an insurance policy:

1. Low premiums

2. Nothing in the small print which you don't understand or which could jeopardise your claim.

3. The option to extend the insurance to outside your home country for free, or a small fee, to cover a trip abroad (the insurance company will normally require prior warning of this).

It should cover:

1. Loss or damage to your windsurfer whether on or off the water.

2. Third party liability to cover accidents on the water.

Your car insurance should cover third party damage should your board fall off the roof during transit. Check this with your car insurance broker before travelling with equipment on your roofrack.

Glossary

Here is a glossary of the windsurfing terms used in this book. For explanations of the words used to describe parts of the board or rig, see pages 4-5. Italicized words are explained elsewhere in the glossary.

Apparent wind Wind which you feel as you are sailing along. A combination of the *true wind*, and wind created by your own speed.

Beach start A way of setting sail from shallow water, without having to *uphaul* the rig.

Beam reach Course whereby the board travels across the wind.

Bear away Steer the board away from the wind.

Bottom turn Turn made at the bottom of a wave, causing you to sail across its face.

Broad reach *Downwind* course between a *beam reach* and a *run*.

Buoyancy aid A light, sleeveless jacket, worn to help you stay afloat if you fall in the water.

Camber inducer A piece of plastic which fits around the mast, holding the batten rigidly in place. Improves the windflow around the sail.

Carve gybe A *gybe* achieved by *footsteering*. The sail flips around the front of the board, and the board carves through the water on its inside *rail*.

Centre of effort (CE) An imaginary point on the sail, where its power is greatest.

Centre of lateral resistance (CLR) The point on the board where resistance to sideways movement is greatest.

Chop Small waves

Close hauled Course whereby you sail as close to the wind as possible.

Close reach *Upwind* course between a *beam reach* and *close hauled*.

Concaves Scoops and curves on the underside of a board.

Course race A race which normally involves sailing around a triangular or 'W' shaped course.

Cross-shore wind A wind blowing parallel to the shore.

Custom board Board made to the specific demands of a sailor.

Cutback A sharp turn made at the top of the wave.

Dirty wind Windflow which has been disturbed by obstacles.

Drain position Stage half-way through *uphauling* the rig, when you allow the water to fall out of the mast tube.

Dry steamer A *steamer* which has seals on it and keeps you 80% dry.

Drysuit Suit which keeps you warm by keeping you dry.

Duck gybe *Gybe* in which the sail flips over your head as the board turns on its inside *rail*.

Duck tack *Tack* which involves ducking under the sail.

Duckspin tack A combination of the *duck tack* and *spin tack*.

Footsteering Steering the board by pressing down on one of your feet.

Freestyling Doing tricks on your board, normally in light winds.

Gybing Turning the back of the board through the wind.

Harness Device worn around the chest, waist or seat. Enables you to hook in to a harness line (attached to the boom), thereby taking the strain off your arms.

Head dip *Freestyle* manoeuvre where you dip your head into the water as you are sailing along.

High jump Wave jump where you concentrate on gaining as much height as possible.

Hypothermia A potentially fatal condition, resulting from over-exposure to the cold.

Leeward side Side furthest away from the wind.

Long john A sleeveless wetsuit.

Long jump Wave jump in which you travel as great a distance lengthwise as possible.

Neoprene A kind of rubber material used to make wetsuits.

No Go Zone Area of around 45° either side of the wind direction, in which it is impossible to sail.

Offshore wind A wind blowing away from the shore.

One-design race A race where only one type of board and rig is allowed.

Onshore wind A wind blowing on to the shore.

Overhand grip Both palms are placed over the top of the boom.

Pirouette *Freestyle* trick where you throw the mast into the wind and spin on the ball of your foot, before grabbing hold of the mast again.

Planing Sailing at such a fast speed that the board skims across the surface of the water rather than ploughing through it.

Port Left. If your left shoulder is closest to the mast, you are sailing on a port tack.

Rail Edge of the board.

Railriding Standing with both feet on the *rail* and the board on its edge as you sail along.

Rigging Assembling the mast, sail and boom ready for sailing.

Rollercoaster Wavesailing techniques, whereby you turn into the wind at the bottom of the wave and sail back up to the top again.

Safety leash A piece of elastic, attaching the rig to the board. Prevents them from becoming separated if the mast foot comes out of the slot or track.

Sail numbers Race numbers attached to your sail for easy identification.

Sailing back to front Sailing with your back towards the sail.

Sailing clew first Sailing with the clew pointing over the front of the board.

Sailing downwind Sailing with the wind behind you.

Sailing upwind Sailing into the wind.

Secure position Positioning of the board, sail and sailor where the board remains stable.

Sheeting in Pulling the sail towards you with your back hand until it is just full of wind.

Slalom race A race involving reaching and *gybing* around a series of marks.

Slam gybe *Gybe* whereby the board pivots on its tail and the sail flips very quickly around the front of the board.

Speed sail A large version of a skateboard with a normal rig attached to it **or** the kind of rig used for *speedsailing*.

Speed sailing Sailing on a speed sail.

Speedsailing Sailing as fast as possible against the clock.

Spin tack *Tack* which involves spinning through 360° whilst moving around the front of the board.

Spin-out A problem which occurs at high speed, caused by too much air getting under the board. The result is that the board slips sideways.

Starboard Right. If your right shoulder is closest to the mast, you are sailing on a starboard tack.

Steamer A winter wetsuit of at least 5mm thickness of *neoprene*.

Tacking Turning the board through the eye of the wind.

Trimming the board Positioning your feet on the board to keep it level or sail it at the angle you require.

True wind The wind you feel if you are standing still.

Uphauling Standing on the board and pulling the rig up from the water.

Upside-down jump Wave jump where the board turns upside down before carrying on to land.

Volume The amount of filling in a board. This effects the board's buoyancy.

Wake Small waves created by the board as it travels through the water. Attached to the back of the board unless the board is *planing*.

Water start A way of setting sail in deep water, without having to stand on the board and *uphaul* the rig.

Wetsuit A suit which keeps you warm by trapping water between your body and the suit.

Wind weapon A combination of a windsurfer and hang glider.

Windshift A change in the direction of the wind.

Windward side Side nearest to the wind.

Index

Acknowledgements

We would like to thank the following individuals and companies who so generously allowed us to reproduce their photographs.

Page 3 (racing): photographer **Gilles Lhotte**

Page 3 (high jump): photographer **Steve Wilkings**

Page 31 (head dip): photographer **Cliff Webb, Evans Webb Associates**

Page 32 (railride): photographer **Cliff Webb, Evans Webb Associates**

Page 33 (tail first on the rail and clew first on the rail):

photograph **Astonocean**, rider **Stuart Sawyer**

Page 34 (body drag): © **Mistral Windsurfing**

Page 35 (duckspin tack): photographer **Alex Williams**

Page 38 (rollercoaster and cutback): photographer **Steve Wilkings**

Page 38 (bottom turn): photographer, **Cliff Webb, Evans Webb Associates**

Page 39 (long jump and upside-down jump): **Cliff Webb, Evans Webb Associates**

Page 39 (high jump): photographer **Steve Wilkings**

Page 42 (racing): photographer: **Gil Lanzi**